D1389433

FAMOUS CHEFS
(AND OTHER CHARACTERS)
COOK WITH BEER

W. SCOTT GRIFFITHS AND
CHRISTOPHER FINCH

LORETTA HWONG–GRIFFITHS, FOOD EDITOR

DOUBLEDAY
NEW YORK   LONDON   TORONTO   SYDNEY   AUCKLAND

Art Direction by Katherine Takahashi
Photography by E. K. Waller
Food Styling by Norman Stewart
Design by R. Patricia Folgar

PUBLISHED BY

DOUBLEDAY

A DIVISION OF

BANTAM DOUBLEDAY

DELL PUBLISHING

GROUP, INC.

1540 BROADWAY,

NEW YORK,

NEW YORK 10036

DOUBLEDAY AND

THE PORTRAYAL OF

AN ANCHOR WITH A

DOLPHIN ARE

TRADEMARKS OF

DOUBLEDAY, A

DIVISION OF

BANTAM DOUBLEDAY

DELL PUBLISHING

GROUP, INC.

LIBRARY OF CONGRESS

CATALOGING–IN–

PUBLICATION DATA

GRIFFITHS, W. SCOTT,

FAMOUS CHEFS (AND

OTHER CHARACTERS)

COOK WITH BEER/

W. SCOTT GRIFFITHS &

CHRISTOPHER FINCH.

P.   CM.

INCLUDES INDEX.

ISBN 0-385-48041-5

1. COOKERY (BEER)

2. BEER. I. FINCH,

CHRISTOPHER II. TITLE.

TX726.3.G75 1996'

641.6'23—DC20

95-26435

CIP

PRINTED IN THE UNITED

STATES OF AMERICA.

MAY 1996

FIRST EDITION

10 9 8 7 6 5 4 3 2 1

TABLE OF CONTENTS

ACKNOWLEDGMENTS

We would like to acknowledge all those whose support, expertise, hard work, and encouragement shaped this project into an anthology of inspirational beer recipes.

Special thanks to those who helped kindle the spirit of this book from the beginning: B. J. Doerfling, who added expertise and guidance on the food editing, Charles and Rose Ann Finkel from Merchant du Vin, Chuck Frank, who recommended many of the top chefs, Elyse Grinstein, a special lady and talented architect, Lucia Hwong—one of our characters who attracted a few of our other characters, John Kaufman—a great restaurant operator, Judith Riven, our agent, Michael Shafer from the Depot, Tamara Thomas, and Tara Thomas from 410 Boyd restaurant.

Our deep thanks to the many breweries who gave generously their time and contributed their beers for our beautiful photography and in preparing the recipes: Brooklyn Brewery, Celis Brewery, Great Lakes Brewery, Hart Brewery, Pike's Place Brewery/Merchant du Vin, Redhook Brewery, Rhino Chasers/William & Scott Brewing Company.

To Katherine Takahashi and Ruth Folgar, for their never wavering pursuit of organization, diligence, and sensitivity to design. To E. K. Waller and Norman Stewart for their food photography and dramatic visual statements.

A round of applause should be given to all the chefs and other characters who contributed recipes, their time, cooperation, and culinary diversity.

In closing, we would like to express gratitude to all the friends of William & Scott.

W. Scott Griffiths
Christopher Finch
Loretta Hwong-Griffiths

Wine gentrifies, beer unifies.

—W. SCOTT GRIFFITHS

INTRODUCTION

This book started with a simple idea. I love great food and I have a passion for great beer. Why not a book on cooking with beer that draws upon the experience of friends and the resources of some of America's finest chefs?

I discussed the idea with my wife, Loretta—who, in my opinion, is one of those great chefs (and who has served as food editor on this project)—and with Christopher Finch (who had collaborated with me on a previous book, *America's Best Beers*). They agreed that it offered a wonderful premise for a cookbook and we went to work right away.

Until a few years ago, Loretta and I were active wine afficionados, collecting mostly the wines of California. We went to wine tastings, cooked with wine, and lived in the world of wine. Then I discovered the American craft beer movement and fell in love with the wonderful brews that were being produced by dedicated men and women from California to Maine—brews that could be compared with the great beers of Europe.

At the time, I headed an advertising/design company that sponsored a softball team. After games, we served beer that bore the label Rhino Chasers™ (named, in fond memory of my youth, for the surfers who hunted big waves with long boards known by that name). This brought me into contact with the microbrewing world, and soon arranged distribution of Rhino Chasers™ Amber Ale to a handful of Los Angeles restaurants. I started going to beer festivals and visiting brewpubs and small breweries all over the country. I was hooked, and in 1990, I founded William & Scott Company, which now offers a full range of Rhino Chasers ales and lagers. The company raised capital, brought in experienced management, and lined up distributors in 200 major American markets. Against stiff competition, it won the right to build a pub that brought craft beers to Los Angeles International Airport.

The idea for a beer cookbook, then, grew out of my passion for quality beer and out of my first-hand observations of powerful trends in the marketplace. Research told me that America had a proud beer heritage, being heir to both the Anglo/Irish ale and stout tradition and the lager tradition that evolved in Germany, Bohemia, and Austria. At the turn of the century, there were more than three thousand small breweries turning out fine beers for local markets all over America.

And beer was used in American kitchens to enhance everything from New England pot roast to chili con carne.

With Prohibition and the industrialization of brewing that followed, all that changed. A few giant brewers dominated the market, swamping America with bland lagers. The idea of cooking with beer was temporarily lost.

Then, in the 1970s and 1980s, a revolution in American brewing began to assert itself. Once again small brewers were crafting varied and satisfying beers for their local markets. Often those beers were served on premises in brewpubs that also sold food. It was natural enough for the chefs in these brewpubs to employ beer in some of their offerings, and so the tradition of cooking with beer began to re-establish itself. Other craft beer fans started to cook with beer at home, and fine beers began to find their way into the best restaurants. Inevitably, some of the most inventive of American chefs began to think about cooking with beer. The idea of cooking with beer began to seem as logical, once again, as cooking with wine.

Originally, the title of this book was to be <u>Our Friends Cook With Beer</u>. Some of those friends happened to be well-known chefs and, in the course of conversation, they mentioned the project to other chefs. Soon we had recipes from an array of acclaimed culinary talent—from old masters like André Soltner to the latest Pacific Rim innovators—that surpassed our wildest expectations. We also received fascinating recipes from interested and interesting amateurs who can only be described as characters. Hence the book's present name.

Loretta, Chris, and I are immensely grateful to everyone who has contributed to this project. We are also astonished at the variety and creativity of their contributions, from Michael Robert's Broiled Salmon with Barbecue Beer Glaze to actress and choreographer Debbie Allen's Honey-Roasted Lamb.

We understood from the beginning that cooking with beer could be a rewarding experience. We are amazed, however, at the adventurous and satisfying range of recipes we have received. It is our privilege to offer these riches to you for your enjoyment.

—W. Scott Griffiths

WHY COOK WITH BEER?

It's strange that there should be any need to deal with the question "Why cook with beer?" The answer ought to be obvious, but the fact is that few people in America do cook with beer, not many beer recipes are found in standard cookbooks, and until recently beer dishes in American restaurants tended to be limited to marginal items such as fish fried in beer batter, and even these were not very common.

Skeptics might argue that perhaps there is a good reason for this neglect of the culinary possibilities of beer, namely the fact that beer does little to enhance food.

Wrong.

Entertaining with Style

TOP: *At the start of the meal, guests toast good food, good beer, and good friends with pale ale, served in this case as an appetizer.*
LEFT: *Charles Finkel looks on as Chef Melissa Flynn adds the finishing touches to Ellensburg lamb marinated in a sauce of Samuel Smith Taddy Porter and fresh organic herbs.*

The fact is that beer can do as much for food as wine, adding its own characteristics to a given dish while at the same time bringing out the best in other ingredients. In Europe, great chefs and housewives alike employ beer as a primary ingredient in a wide variety of dishes, and as a flavoring agent in many others. Carbonnade—a robust beef stew that uses beer as its base—is the national dish of Flemish Belgium. Other traditional favorites range from Danish breakfast beer soup (complete with eggs and whipped cream) to Scots gingerbread flavored with the strong, dark ale known in Scotland as "a wee heavy." For centuries, the English have stewed eels in beer and have used ale to marinate venison (enhancing the gamy meat with a maltiness that makes for an unforgettable taste experience). Finnish wives cook the local crayfish with dill and a mixture of beer and vodka, and Swedes rave about a dish called Hokarepanna (coachman's pan) in which layers of lamb kidneys, pork, sliced onions, and sliced potatoes are simmered in a broth generously laced with ale. Not surprisingly, the Germans cook extensively with beer and are especially adept at using it to flavor specialty meats and sausages. Irish chefs have been known to braise salmon in porter, and French brasseries sometimes serve a stew known as ragout à la Irlandaise, which employs Guinness stout as its distinguishing ingredient.

Why, then, has beer not come to play a more prominent place in the American kitchen? Americans, after all, consume their fair share of beer, and since the sixties at least have been willing to experiment with all kinds of exotic cuisines and new ingredients.

In all probability, the reason for this neglect of beer in the kitchen owes a good deal to the fact that—until quite recently—most American beer was so bland and characterless that it had become a mere thirst quencher. The thought that it might have an affinity for food, other than hot dogs, was almost comical.

The insipid brews produced by the big breweries belied the fact that beer has a proud tradition on this side of the Atlantic. Beer came to America with the Pilgrim Fathers, and for centuries British-style beers—especially ales and porters—dominated the American brewing scene. (George Washington and several other signatories of the

A Beer Dinner

❈

The last thing we want to be held responsible for is setting down pedantic rules about specific beers that should accompany specific foods, or suggesting that if your main course is braised in beer, you should use beer as an ingredient in every course, from appetizer to dessert. Cooking with beer should not be consigned to a culinary ghetto. A great beer-based dish fits into any meal, whatever the other courses. And where serving beer with food is concerned, the rules are there to be broken. It is traditional that oysters on the half shell are served with stout or porter. They taste wonderful that way, but they're not half bad when washed down with a really good, crisp pilsner.

That said, many beer lovers will be tempted to invite friends to a meal in which only beer-based dishes are served and for which a range of beers is the only accompaniment. The recipes in this book provide the opportunity to plan any number of entirely beer-based meals. The host will then be faced with the enjoyable task of selecting beers to accompany those meals.

Clearly, a dish cooked with stout can appropriately be accompanied by stout (or perhaps by that delectable concoction known as Black Velvet, consisting of three-parts stout to one-part champagne). Similarly a salad made with a dressing that uses Framboise—a Belgian raspberry-flavored lambic beer—can properly be washed down with Framboise.

There is no need to be rigid about any of this, but some general guide lines are worth keeping in mind if one is planning a meal in which the accompanying beers are going to be orchestrated from apéritif to after-dinner drink.

The beer apéritif is an often misunderstood category. Few people think of beer as an apéritif at all, but in fact there are certain kinds of stronger beer that can be asked to perform much the same duty as fortified wines such as sherry. A well-attenuated German bock, such as the classic Einbecker Ur-Bock, makes a fine apéritif, comparable to a dryish sherry on the rocks. Some of the maltier Bavarian bocks are equivalent to cream sherries. Certain beer afficionados recommend strong Belgian ales—Duvel, for instance, and the Trappist abbey ales—as apéritifs. They certainly whet the appetite, but they are very heady drinks and if served before a meal they should be meted out in small quantities (6 ounces to the glass).

Other lighter possibilities for use as an apéritif, especially in warm weather, are the more characterful wheat beers, both imported and domestic. Among the latter, Celis White—produced in Texas by a Belgian master brewer—is outstanding, with something of the herbal spiciness of the best wine-based apéritifs. Another superb example is Tabernash Weiss, produced by the Colorado Brewing Company of Denver, but any good hefe-weizen will serve the purpose.

So far as opening courses are concerned, generally light bodied beers are called for, though this does not mean *that they have to be pallid in flavor. With a terrine of duck livers, for example, you might call on something with pronounced character to challenge the assertiveness of the pâté. A French farmhouse ale like Jenlain would make a perfect match, but the terrine will taste just as good with any of several American amber beers, both ales (Rhino Chasers Amber Ale) and lagers (New Amsterdam Amber).*

As already noted, oysters have an affinity for stout and porter. Other shellfish, and seafood in general, tend to match up most readily with good pale lagers—from Pilsner Urquell to any of the many good American craft-brewed pale lagers. But don't be afraid to serve a light ale with seared tuna or a dish of little neck clams, and a glass of dark wheat beer does wonders for trout.

As an accompaniment to poultry, pale lagers are always appropriate, but a Red Tail Ale or a Boston Stock Ale will do much to enhance roast duck. And when it comes to game birds, try one of the higher gravity British or American ales (Young's Special London Ale, perhaps, or Redhook IPA). The vinous character of these stronger, top-fermented beers, enhances the richness of all game, both furred and feathered.

Pork and veal both match up well with pale lagers, though the best in some veal dishes is brought out by the richer tastes of various ales and amber lagers. As for red meat, it is usually at its best with the more vinous ales and the chewier reddish and dark lagers. An exception to this rule must be made for highly spiced dishes, such as chile con carne, which call for pale lagers to cool the palate.

Ham goes well with most beers, but it is especially well complemented by the remarkable "smoked" beers produced in Franconia, a region of Northern Bavaria that has yet to be discovered by the great majority of American beer enthusiasts. One "smoked" beer—Kaiserdom—is occasionally found on this side of the Atlantic, and it is worth seeking out. As an accompaniment to food it goes equally well with ham, cheese, and savory dishes of all kinds.

Cheese responds to any of the more assertive beers—Anchor Steam Beer, good British and American ales, Irish stout, Yankee porter, or Bavarian bock. As for dessert beers—a bizarre idea for many people—the fruit-flavored lambics of Belgium are ideal, and there are now many excellent American fruit-flavored beers that fill the same role.

After dinner, stout goes splendidly with coffee, and there are a number of beers that can be substituted for port or brandy. The strong, sweet, malty Bavarian doppelbocks are the ports of the beer world. Belgium's Trappist abbey ales (already noted as possible apéritifs) are more brandy-like, as are the so-called barley wines that are the powerhouses of the British and American ale tradition. For good American examples, try Sierra Nevada's Bigfoot or Anchor Brewing's Old Foghorn.

It should be noted that, when serving beer with a meal, traditional beer glasses are not always appropriate. German lager glasses work well enough as part of a smart table setting, but British tankards are apt to look decidedly clumsy. Consider serving your beers in wine glasses. After-dinner snorts, such as barley wine, can be served in brandy snifters. ∾

Declaration of Independence brewed beer for their own use, and sometimes for commercial distribution too.) American cooks of the period used these British-style brews in their recipes, boiling lobster in ale and blending porter with bourbon and other ingredients to make a gravy to go over game. Later, German and Central European brewers brought lager beers to the New World so that, from the mid-nineteenth century till World War I, America could boast one of the widest selections of beer styles to be found anywhere.

Prohibition put an end to that, destroying the majority of those small American breweries that once assured our cities of that wide range of beer styles. In the post-Prohibition era, industrialized brewing replaced variety, with many brands that all aspired to a single style— a weak apology for pilsner beer that was the liquid equivalent of packaged white bread.

Around 1980, however, American beer lovers began to fight back. Importers like Merchant du Vin in Seattle began to seek out fine European beers that had long been unavailable in the American marketplace, and more importantly still, small American brewers like the Anchor brewery in San Francisco, Sierra Nevada in Northern California, and Redhook in Seattle spearheaded a renaissance of craft brewing that continues to this day.

The revival started on the West Coast, but by the late 1980s it had spread to most parts of the country and today it is especially strong in New England, the Midwest, and the Southwest, as well as in California and the Northwest. Today there are well over 400 craft breweries—including brewpubs—operating in the U.S.A. and beers such as Rhino Chasers™ and some others are now widely distributed and can be found in supermarkets and convenience stores as well as specialty outlets. As in pre-Prohibition days, ales and porters, stouts, pilsners, and bocks are now available from coast to coast.

In particular these craft beers are finding their way into many of America's best restaurants. Customers have discovered that quality beer can be much more than just a refreshing beverage. Properly chosen, it makes a splendid accompaniment to a wide variety of foods. There is no better way of enhancing oysters on the half shell than by washing them down with a glass of creamy stout or porter. A mellow India Pale Ale goes as well with roast beef as any fine claret, and when it comes to Far Eastern cuisines—Indian, Thai, Chinese, Japanese—a crisp pilsner is almost always preferable to wine. Certain beers, such as bocks and strong "winter warmer" ales, can properly be served as aperitifs or after-dinner drinks.

The fact—now widely accepted—that fine beers go well with fine foods should be a clue to the fact that fine beers are well worth cooking with because they offer a world of flavors that cannot be attained in any other way. They can be used to add zest to down-home favorites—New England pot roasts, Cajun shrimp, chili—or they can be used in more eclectic and creative ways.

TOP: *Food editor Loretta Griffiths enjoys a German wheat beer, zesty with sedimentary yeast.*

BOTTOM: *For dessert, Bosc pears poached in Lindemans Peche, served with fresh figs and a Peche lambic sorbet.*

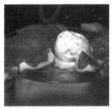

WHY COOK WITH BEER?

Beer Tasting Tips

❖

If you're thinking of having a beer tasting party, these are a few things to keep in mind:

1 / *If your guests are relative novices where craft beers are concerned, you might want to serve half-a-dozen different styles of beer (ales, stouts, pilsners, etc.) in order to familiarize the tasters with the range of brews available in today's market. If your guests are already fans of craft beers, it's more usual to make the tasting a comparison of brews in the same style. If, for example, you are tasting British-style pale ales, you might select three imports (Bass, Fuller's London Pride, and Samuel Smith Old Brewery Pale Ale, for example) and three domestic brands (such as Sierra Nevada Pale Ale, Liberty Ale, and Rhino Chasers American Ale). Six is about the right number of brews for a serious tasting.*

2 / *If you want this to be a blind test, pour the beers in a room away from your guests, about 3 to 4 ounces to a glass. This way, one standard 12-ounce bottle of each beer will be enough for every three or four guests. Wine glasses are ideal for beer tastings. Their stems allow them to be handled without contaminating the bowl in a way that would interfere with the appearance of the beer. For a blind test, the base of each glass can be coded with adhesive labels.*

3 / *If this a serious tasting, provide a spit bucket. If the beers are consumed, the alcohol from the first brews will*

It is generally understood when cooking with wine that different families of wine serve different purposes. You don't ask a Muscadet to do the work of a Pommard, or vice versa. Very much the same is true of cooking with beer. You will get very different results if you interpret a recipe that simply calls for beer as meaning pilsner, on the one hand, or doppelbock on the other. Both these beers are styles of lager, but they differ greatly in malt and hop character. Substitute other members of the beer family, and the same will be true.

An experiment will show how different styles of beer can weave their distinctive kinds of magic when used in cooking. Perhaps the simplest of all classic dishes involving beer is Welsh rarebit. There are many variations on the basic recipe, but essentially Welsh rarebit—which is served on toast—consists of grated cheese (preferably a sharp Cheddar) and butter, melted over *influence the way tasters respond to the later brews.*

4 / *Serve the beers one at a time. They should be judged according to the following criteria: a: Appearance (clarity, color, beading, etc.), b: Aroma, c: Flavor, d: Balance, e: Finish, g: Overall impression.*

5 / *Each taster should be provided with a score card on which points can be assigned according to these criteria. A good system assigns up to three points for appearance, three for aroma, four for flavor, three for balance, three for finish, and four for overall impression. Space should be left for general remarks about positive and negative qualities such as a good hop character, excessive carbonation, etc.*

6 / *After the beers have been served singly, an opportunity should be provided for comparisons to be made. One way to do this is for the host to bring disguised sample bottles into the tasting room. The wife of one beer fancier we know has knitted "cozys" that can be slipped over bottles to conceal their identity, but wrapping the bottles in dish towels or cloth napkins will do just as well. Aluminum foil can also make an excellent disguise.*

7 / *After the formal tasting, add up the scores, allow guests to read their scorecard remarks or make comments, then pour the same beers for general consumption and let the arguments commence.*

a low heat, moistened with beer, thickened with a little flour, and made savory with dry mustard, Worcestershire sauce, pepper, and other condiments to taste.

The amount of beer called for is typically no more than 2 tablespoons to a serving, but the style of beer used can have a considerable effect on the results. If a hoppy pale ale is employed, the bitterness of the hops will heighten the sharpness of the cheese to make for a delightfully zesty, almost pungent flavor. A sweet stout (such as Mackeson), on the other hand, will produce a richer and mellower result. In either case, the rarebit will be delicious, but the point is that the character of the dish is altered according to the beer that has been chosen.

Given that there are more than twenty basic styles of beer (by the most conservative estimate), and hundreds of variants within the parameters of the more popular styles, the wide

*After an impeccable
meal, guests enjoy
hand-made cigars
and hand-crafted
beers as mellow
and rewarding as
vintage port or
old Armagnac.*

range of flavors to be attained by cooking with beer can easily be imagined. Beer-based marinades alone can add enormously to the culinary spectrum.

There are some rules that must be observed, of course. Because barley malt is so sweet, most high-quality beers contain significant quantities of hops (derived from the female cone of the hop vine), which help to clarify and preserve the brew, to add aroma, and most importantly to provide the bitterness that balances the sugariness of the malt and makes for a pleasingly dry beverage.

In cooking, that bitterness—if it is not allowed for—can cause problems. Classic beer dishes, such as the Carbonnade of Flanders, offset for this hoppy tartness with caramelized onions, or some comparably sweet ingredient.

The occasional difficulties of cooking with beer, however, are greatly outweighed by the advantages. Beer has a kinship for hearty and strongly flavored foods—such as game and smoked or highly spiced meats that overpower all but the most robust of wines. Yet beer can be used in delicate dishes too, such as shrimp or crawfish braised in pilsner. And, whether used in delicate or hearty dishes, beer adds no calories to the meal since the calorie-bearing alcohol evaporates during the cooking process, leaving only the flavor behind.

And ultimately, it is that flavor—or those flavors—that justify cooking with beer. Before starting, however, it is worth learning a little bit about the different styles of beer, because it's as important to understand the difference between brown ale and bock as it is to understand the difference between olive oil and peanut oil.

THE BEER FAMILIES

*E*xcept for a few specialties, such as wheat beer and fruit-flavored beer, all great beers are made from just four basic ingredients—barley malt, water, yeast, and hops.

The barley malt is the basic fermentable material (equivalent to the grape in the case of wine) and provides the primary flavor of the brew. It is mashed in water, the resulting mixture being known—after it has been clarified—as the *wort*. Hops are then added to the wort, after which it is boiled in the brew kettle. (This is the actual brewing process.) Further clarified and cooled, the wort is then fermented through the agency of yeast, which is pitched into the fermenting vessel. After the brew

Draft Beers

*Tap handles like this are a symbol
of quality beer, since a brew that has been
cask conditioned must be carefully pumped by
hand (as opposed to pasteurized keg
beers which are usually dispensed
by electric pump). Tap handles also offer an
opportunity for designers to help give beer its
brand identity. (Tap handle courtesy of
Rhino Chasers·)*

has fermented for the appropriate time, it is aged in conditioning tanks. (Sometimes more hops are added at this phase to add fragrance.)

Within this basic process, however, the brewer has options, and even the basic ingredients come in many forms. There are different types of barley, for instance, and the barley—malted or not—can be roasted to various degrees, which will produce brews that vary in darkness and flavor. Different water sources provide assorted trace elements of salts and minerals, which affect the character of the brew. Yeast cultures are of two basic kinds—top fermenting and bottom fermenting—but vary greatly from brewery to brewery. Hops come in many varieties, each of which has its own distinctive profile in terms of both dryness and aroma. (American hops, for example, tend to be more floral than European varieties.)

A master brewer can take these four basic ingredients and orchestrate them in many ways. A Rhino Chasers® American Ale may differ from a German alt beer, for instance, as a string quartet by Samuel Barber differs from a string quartet by Beethoven.

The basic styles of beer fall into two families (though there are a couple of anomalies). The ale family—much the older of the two—consists of brews that are fermented at near room temperature using yeasts that rise to the top of the wort during the fermentation process. The lager family is made up of brews that are fermented and aged at very cool temperatures using yeast that sinks to the bottom of the wort.

There was a time when virtually all beers belonged to the ale family. The lager family did not come into its own until the nineteenth century, when industrial refrigeration and advances in brewing science made it possible to produce bottom-fermented beers that were at the time remarkable for their clarity and long shelf life. As a general rule, ales tend to be richer and fruitier—more vinous—than lagers. Lagers—especially the lighter colored pilsners and helles—tend to be crisp and refreshing (though there are significant exceptions).

The following are the principal members of the two major beer families, with some of the characteristics that have bearing on their use in the kitchen. The brand-name beers we have selected as

The American Craft Brewing Renaissance

❖

Little more than twenty years ago, America was a wilderness so far as quality brewing was concerned. On the East Coast, a few good beers such as Ballantine IPA and Prior Double Dark had somehow survived Prohibition and the rage for "rationalized" brewing that followed (for "rationalized" read "more profits, less flavor"). On the West Coast, Fritz Maytag had performed a public service by rescuing Anchor Steam beer from bankruptcy, and restoring the company to fiscal health. In between, "rationalization" ruled and the bulk of the American public was brainwashed into believing that good beer had more to do with frosty mugs than with the artistry that a great brewmaster brings to blending malt and hops.

Not everyone had been brainwashed by Madison Avenue, however. American troops stationed in Germany discovered that not all beers had to taste like those they found in the supermarkets at home. Tourists visiting England and Ireland discovered that the myths about warm beer were greatly exaggerated and that the ales and stouts of the old world offered unsuspected pleasures that the brewing moguls of Milwaukee and St. Louis did not seem to want Americans to know about.

Back in America, inspired by Maytag's example, some of these former servicemen and tourists—and other determined real beer lovers and ex-home brewers—began to think about the possibility of importing those great beer tastes from Europe or, better still, reproducing them on this side of the Atlantic. Men like Jack McAuliffe, Michael Leybourn, Ken Grossman, and Paul Camusi in California, Charles Finkel, Bert Grant, and Paul Shipman in Washington, and Bill Newman in New York contributed to the beginnings of the revolution, importing fine beers in the case of Finkel and launching craft breweries and brewpubs in the case of the others.

It was a revolution that spread like a California wild fire fanned by a Santa Ana wind. Soon there were a dozen craft brewers, then a score, then a hundred. People who follow trends said that the craft brewing revolution would have to peak soon. But before anyone had the time to absorb this information there were two hundred craft breweries, then three hundred, then four. Once awakened, the American appetite for quality beer seemed to know no bounds and even the brewing giants began to take notice, marketing their own approximations of craft beers and buying into craft beer companies.

Things have reached the point where mainstream hotel lounges and airport bars all over the country have craft beers on their menu. Americans have learned the difference between a porter and a pilsner. Pizza parlors and pioneers of Pacific Rim cuisine alike offer the great beers of America and the great beers of the world.

It is against this background that we invite readers to join in the new adventure of cooking with beer. ❧

representative of various styles were chosen from those that are most widely available. If your local micro's house speciality, or a favorite import, is not listed, that does not mean we do not recommend it, but we don't want to send readers from Chicago chasing after a beer that is available only in Burlington, Vermont.

TOP-FERMENTED BEERS (ALES)

BITTER / This is the basic draft ale of the British pub—and increasingly of many American brewpubs—a hearty, malty brew that typically is generously hopped and relatively low in carbonation. Bitter would make a splendid general-purpose cooking beer, but in its genuine draft form it is seldom available in the home. Fortunately pale ale serves exactly the same culinary purpose.

PALE ALE / Pale ale is the bottled equivalent of bitter, and fine imported and domestic versions of this classic brew are widely available. "Pale" is a relative term, first used in England when the most popular beer there was porter, a licorice-colored brew. Typically, pale ales are deep golden or reddish in color; they can be amber or chestnut. The finest-quality pale ales are sometimes called India Pale Ales (IPAs), recalling the days when they were shipped to the Far East, maturing during the course of the voyage. Pale ales are well hopped and rich in flavor, with fruity, vinous overtones. Their balance makes them perhaps the most useful of all beers when it comes to cooking.

MILD / This is another form of draft ale, still popular in some regions of the British Isles and occasionally experimented with by American brewmasters. Less hoppy than bitter, this would be a fine beer to cook with but, like bitter, it is essentially a pub beer and so is seldom available to the home chef.

BROWN ALE / Brown ale probably originated as the bottled version of the classic dark style of mild. Increasingly popular in America, brown ale has a rich, malty character that is well suited to hearty dishes such as stews.

SCOTCH ALE / A strong, dark ale that chefs should approach with caution because it is both intensely malty and extremely bitter. If its properties are understood, however, it can add a great deal of character to food.

BARLEY WINE / A very strong, heady style of ale—the equivalent of fortified wines such as sherry and port—which can make an outstanding contribution to food if it is handled with care.

PORTER / A black-as-molasses brew that was immensely popular in Britain and America during the eighteenth and nineteenth centuries, porter has recently enjoyed a revival and is now readily available in many parts of the country. For drinking purposes, the classic bitter versions are preferable. For cooking purposes, however, the sweeter versions are often more manageable, since they lend an almost espresso-like toastiness to a dish without problems of tartness.

STOUT / A creamier, more full-bodied version of porter, stout exaggerates both the advantages and disadvantages of its close cousin. Anyone cooking with stout should be aware that there is a huge difference between dry, bitter versions such as Guinness and sweet versions such as Mackeson's. American stouts—and there are many of them—vary from the very bitter to the fairly sweet. If you are cooking with a stout that is unfamiliar to you, taste it first. That way you can avoid disappointments.

BELGIAN ALES / Along with Britain, Belgium is the country most associated with the survival of the ale tradition. Belgium's ales are even more varied than those of the British Isles and are often extremely vinous in character. They are not as widely imitated in America as British ales, although a handful of American breweries do produce remarkably good Belgian-style ales. These brews are so idiosyncratic that it's foolish to generalize about them. Properly understood they are wonderful to cook with, but it's advisable to familiarize oneself with the properties of the individual beers (by tasting) before using them in the kitchen.

TRAPPIST ALES / Brewed in Trappist abbeys—though they have many commercial imitators—these are among the finest of the Belgian ales. The most prized examples are world classics. High in alcohol content, they have much in common with barley wine.

ALTBIER / The German equivalent of ale, altbier can be substituted for pale ale in many recipes, and is especially suitable for dishes such as those versions of sauerbraten in which the meat is marinated in beer and spices, rather than wine vinegar and spices.

WHEAT BEER / Wheat beers are popular in Germany and Belgium, and increasingly in America. Traditionally they are made from mashes in which wheat is mixed with the barley malt, then fermented like ales through the intervention of top-fermenting yeast. Some American wheat beers, however, are made with lager yeast.

BOTTOM-FERMENTED BEERS (LAGERS)

PILSNER / Named for the town of Pilsen in the Czech Republic, pilsner (sometimes called *pilsener,* or just *pils*) is the world's most popular style of beer—light in color, crisp, and hoppy. Superbly thirst quenching, pilsner is not necessarily the ideal beer to cook with, being relatively light in malt character and distinctively bitter, but it does have its uses.

HELLES / Bavarian-style light-colored lager that is thirst quenching but not as dry as pilsner. It is a good general-purpose cooking beer, somewhat equivalent to pale ale.

MUNCHNER / The dark beer of Bavaria (often called *dunkel*)—malty and sweetish—very good to cook with.

VIENNA / In Europe, reddish lagers are often described as being Viennese in style. In America, this kind of brew is often described as just plain amber beer. Deriving its color and flavor from roasted barley malt, amber beer is extremely useful in the kitchen, lending character to foods without causing complications.

BOCK / A strong form of lager, very valuable in cooking if used with care.

DOPPELBOCK / An even stronger form of lager, notable for its pronounced, sweet malt character.

OTHER STYLES

LAMBIC / Lambics make up a special category of wheat beer that is produced only in Belgium and is spontaneously fermented by natural yeasts in the atmosphere. Some lambics are flavored with fruits such as cherries (*kriek*) or raspberries (*framboise*) and these are especially useful in preparing certain desserts.

FRUIT-FLAVORED BEERS / In recent years, many American craft brewers have experimented with blending fruit flavors with beer. Usually the base is an American-style wheat beer.

STEAM BEER / So-called steam beer (there is no convincing explanation for the name) is an American invention, a style of brew that became famous in California and elsewhere west of the Rockies in the nineteenth century. Fermented with lager yeasts, but at ale temperatures, steam beer combines the freshness of lager with the fruitiness of ale. Having single-handedly kept the style alive, the Anchor Brewery of San Francisco has trademarked the name. In cooking, this splendid beer can be substituted for pale ale.

PRACTICAL ADVICE ABOUT BEER & COOKING

Notes from Christopher

When cooking with beer, the quality of the brew will have an effect on the end product. This means that you should cook with the best examples available of any given style. It's also important to remember that beer is perishable and should be handled and stored with care, otherwise it will disappoint, whether intended for drinking or cooking purposes.

Beer does not respond well to being jolted or shaken since any agitation can trigger chemical changes that will have a deleterious effect on the taste and aroma of the brew. Try to avoid driving around all day with a case of beer in the trunk. If that's unavoidable, give the beer a day or two to settle after you get it home. Some beer connoisseurs will go so far as to avoid storing bottles in the door shelves of refrigerators since the opening and closing of the door can cause enough movement to unbalance some beers.

Exposure to light can also detrimentally alter the chemistry of beer. This is why beer is usually found in green or brown bottles, which offer some protection, but ideally beer should be stored in a dark place where light contamination can be entirely avoided.

The chemistry of beer is also subject to the influence of temperature. Left at room temperature for any length of time—unless your idea of room temperature is significantly below 70°F.—most beers will begin to deteriorate even if stored in the dark. Unless you have a wine cellar, you are best advised to keep your craft beers in a refrigerator at a temperature in the region of 45°F. to 50°F. degrees. Occasionally the brewers of some complex European ales will suggest, on the bottle, that their beer should not be kept in the refrigerator. These brewers must be presumed to be unfamiliar with American domestic arrangements. Unless, once again, you are lucky enough to have a cool wine cellar (or perhaps a cool garage during the winter months)—

you will be better off storing these ales in the fridge.

Except for a few specialty brews—such as the lambics and certain strong ales—beers do not improve with time. In fact they begin to deteriorate quite quickly, even when stored under near ideal conditions. They should, therefore, be purchased from a retail outlet with a quick turnover, and they should be used as soon as possible after purchase. As a general rule, ales are more volatile than lagers and therefore have a shorter shelf life. Stronger brews—whether ales or lagers—tend to have a longer life.

Certain craft beers, such as French "farmhouse" ales, are sold in champagne-style bottles with wired corks. These can be stored horizontally, but all other beers should be stored vertically to avoid contamination from the metal of the cap.

It's still all too commonplace to find, in American bars, good beers being served at sub-polar temperatures in glasses coated with ice. The tradition of the frosty mug is born of the fact that most mainstream American beers aren't worth tasting in the first place. Icy temperatures mask the flavor of beer and therefore do nothing to enhance the enjoyment of quality craft beers.

This is not to say that beers should never be cooled; it's just a matter of not overdoing it. As a general rule, a good lager will taste at its best when served at around 50°F. A pale ale will be at its best when it's a little warmer, about 55°F., which doesn't mean that you would be committing a crime against nature if you served it at 50°F. on a scorching summer afternoon. Common sense comes into play. Bitter stouts like Guinness are often served at near room temperature in Ireland and the United Kingdom, yet they can be surprisingly refreshing, and still flavorful, when served at between 50°F. and 55°F., as is attested by the popularity of such brews in the Caribbean and tropical Asia.

This applies to beers for drinking purposes, of course. Cooking with beer is another matter and here it is important to start with beer that is at room temperature. If you use chilled beer there will be a loss of flavor. If the beer has been refrigerated, therefore, try to take it out at least an hour or two before using. It also makes sense to open the beer some time before it will be used because beer can be more accurately measured once it becomes "flat," and carbonation does nothing to enhance the flavor of the food.

It is the barley malt that provides most of the flavor, when cooking with beer. Yeast and hops can modify that flavor, but it's worth repeating that alcohol plays no role in the equation since it evaporates during the cooking process, leaving neither calories nor the ability to intoxicate.

Notes from Loretta

Food editor Loretta Hwong-Griffiths offers the following hints and reminders when cooking with beer:

1 / Always consider the balance of ingredients within a given dish. Since beer is made with hops, you will need to offset the natural bitterness with sweetening agents. Significant amounts of sugar occur naturally in vegetables such as onions, leeks, shallots, carrots, and corn, and also in fruits. If you are not using enough of these sweetening agents in your recipe, you may need to add honey, molasses, sugar, or malted barley.

2 / In considering the balance of beer dishes remember that acid—from ingredients such as tomatoes, lemon, lime, wine vinegar, and mustard—will offset the natural sweeteners and should be taken into account.

3 / The palate tends to sense sweetness before bitterness. It is important to remember this when tasting beer dishes in order to adjust the balance.

4 / Just using beer as a substitute for some other ingredient is not enough. Ales, stouts, pilsners, and other brews should be used to enhance dishes and lend them a unique character.

5 / Beer is great for robust dishes where its assertive flavor is especially welcome, but it can also be successfully used in subtle dishes, so long as it is employed in moderation.

6 / Beer is extremely useful when cooking game, since it emphasizes the richness of the meat yet at the same time cuts excessive gaminess.

7 / Fish, meats, and poultry are all improved when marinated in beer.

8 / Remember that the flavor of beer is greatly intensified as you reduce the liquid in the pan.

9 / When used with cheese or cream, beer serves the very useful purpose of tempering the richness.

10 / When mixed with flour, beer gives off one of the most wonderful aromas in the food world. For this reason, beer bread, beer pancakes, beer fritters, and other related items, are as enjoyable to cook as they are to eat.

11 / The following ingredients are among those most often used when cooking with beer:

lime juice	chicken stock
lemon juice	beef stock
wine vinegar	veal stock
Worcestershire sauce	Tabasco sauce
cumin	tomatoes
cayenne pepper	onions
chile peppers (all types)	garlic
maple syrup	carrots
honey	bell peppers (red & green)
molasses	barley malt
cilantro	sugar
parsley	corn syrup

Starters

*A fine ale or a great bock can be as satisfying as a hearty soup,
so it is hardly surprising that creative chefs have long delighted in creating
beer-based soups in which the nutty sweetness of malted barley is used to
coax unexpected resonances from a variety of ingredients.
Beer can also contribute greatly to the character of a wide range of
appetizers, whether used as a marinade for shrimp or crawfish, employed
to complement the piquancy of specialty sausages, or called upon as the
catalyst for a folk classic such as Welsh rarebit.*

CHEESE AND CORN SOUP WITH SPAETZLE

4 TO 6 SERVINGS

German spaetzle, or dumplings, have been paired with cheese for generations. In this variation they are flavored with cornmeal and nutmeg to complement a hearty Cheddar and sweet corn soup.

2	medium onions, *coarsely chopped*
2	tablespoons olive oil or butter
2	cups fresh corn kernels
2	(12-ounce) bottles Rhino Chasers® American Amber Ale
2	cups chicken stock or water
	Salt and freshly ground white pepper, to taste
5	tablespoons all-purpose flour
¼	cup yellow cornmeal
¼	teaspoon baking powder
⅛	teaspoon ground nutmeg
2	egg whites
1	pound sharp Cheddar cheese, *grated*

In a large saucepan, sauté the onions in the oil or butter over medium heat about 10 minutes, stirring occasionally. Add the corn kernels and cook 5 minutes longer. Stir in the ale, stock, and salt and pepper to taste and bring to a boil. Reduce the heat, cover, and simmer for 10 minutes. Let cool slightly and transfer to a blender or food processor. Puree (in batches if necessary) just until chunky. Pour back into the saucepan; cover and set aside.

To make the spaetzle, bring a large pot of water to a boil. In a medium bowl, combine the flour, cornmeal, ½ teaspoon salt, ¼ teaspoon white pepper, the baking powder and nutmeg. Add the egg whites and, with an electric mixer, beat at medium speed for about 1 minute.

Drop the dough by ½ teaspoonfuls into the boiling water several at a time, being careful not to crowd the pot. Reduce the heat to a simmer and cook 1 to 2 minutes longer once the dumplings rise to the top. Remove with slotted spoon and drain on paper towels.

Reheat the soup mixture. Add the cheese and cook over low heat, stirring, until the cheese is melted. To serve, rewarm the spaetzle in a preheated 250°F. oven if necessary and arrange in soup bowls. Ladle the hot soup into the bowls.

If Rhino Chasers® American Amber Ale is not available, see Substitution Chart.

PUREED WHITE BEAN AND DARK ALE SOUP

6 TO 10 SERVINGS

*Here is a pureed bean soup without cream
that can be prepared in advance.*

1	medium onion, *chopped*
1	medium shallot, *chopped*
2	medium cloves garlic, *minced*
1	tablespoon olive oil
2	quarts vegetable stock or water
1	cup white beans, *presoaked overnight and drained*
1	large boiling potato, *peeled and diced*
¾	cup Samuel Adams® Dark Ale
1 to 2	sprigs fresh thyme
	Juice of 1 lemon (about 3 tablespoons)
	Salt and freshly ground pepper, to taste
2	tomatoes, *peeled, seeded, and diced*, for garnish (optional)
	Cilantro leaves, for garnish (optional)

In a large saucepot, over medium-high heat, sauté the onion, shallot, and garlic in the olive oil until soft. Add the vegetable stock or water, the beans, the potato, ½ cup of the ale, and the thyme. Bring to a boil. Reduce the heat and simmer, covered, for 1 hour, or until the beans are tender. Remove and discard the thyme. Let cool slightly. In a blender or food processor, puree the mixture in batches until smooth. Strain the soup through a sieve back into the saucepot. Add the remaining ¼ cup of ale, the lemon juice, salt, and pepper and heat through. To serve, ladle into serving bowls and garnish with tomato and cilantro leaves, if desired.

If Samuel Adams® Ale is not available, see Substitution Chart.

WILD RHINO SOUP

6 TO 10 SERVINGS

*The pièce de résistance in this exotic blend is the juxtaposition
of crunchy peanuts in a smooth soup base.*

TAMARA THOMAS

PRESIDENT,
FINE ARTS SERVICES, INC.
LOS ANGELES, CA

2	medium onions, *chopped*
4 to 6	cloves garlic, *minced*
2 to 3	tablespoons vegetable oil
2	tablespoons butter
½	cup chopped celery
½	cup chopped carrots
1	teaspoon chili powder
1	teaspoon curry powder
1	teaspoon ground cumin
	Dash of cayenne pepper
1	(12-ounce) bottle Rhino Chasers® American Amber Ale
5	cups chicken stock or broth
4	medium tomatoes, *peeled, seeded, and chopped*
2	medium boiling potatoes, *peeled and diced* (about 2 cups)
½	cup heavy cream
	Salt and freshly ground pepper, to taste
	Chopped roasted peanuts, for garnish
	Chopped cilantro leaves, for garnish

In a large saucepot, over medium heat, sauté the onions and garlic in the oil and butter just
until tender, about 5 minutes. Add the celery and carrots and cook 2 to 3 minutes longer. Stir
in the spices and cook 1 minute longer. Pour in the ale and bring to a boil. Add the chicken
stock, tomatoes, and potatoes. Return to a boil. Reduce the heat, partially cover, and simmer
about 45 minutes. Let cool slightly. In a blender or food processor, puree the mixture in several
batches. Return the soup to the saucepot and reheat. Whisk in the cream just before serving.
Season with salt and pepper to taste. Ladle into serving bowls and sprinkle with chopped
peanuts and cilantro.

If Rhino Chasers® American Amber Ale is not available, see Substitution Chart.

*Note:
The soup can be
prepared ahead and
refrigerated. Just reheat
and add the cream
before serving.*

KIRIN CHEDDAR CHOWDER WITH WILD RICE

6 TO 8 SERVINGS

Wild rice is not a true rice. It is the seed of a wild marsh grass originally harvested by Indians near the Great Lakes. The nuttiness of wild rice and the hoppiness of beer help temper the richness of the cheese.

6	tablespoons unsalted butter
½	cup diced onion
½	cup diced celery
½	cup diced carrots
1 ½	cups julienned fresh shiitake mushroom caps (*see Note*)
6	tablespoons all-purpose flour
2 ½	cups chicken stock or broth
1	(12-ounce) bottle Kirin® beer
4	ounces sharp Cheddar cheese, *grated*
1	cup heavy cream
1	cup cooked wild rice
1	teaspoon salt
½	teaspoon Worcestershire sauce
¼	teaspoon freshly ground white pepper
⅛	teaspoon Tabasco sauce
½	bunch chives, *thinly sliced,* for garnish

Note:
To substitute dried shiitake mushrooms, place about 15 dried mushrooms in enough boiling water to cover. Let stand 30 minutes. Drain; remove and discard the stems. Slice the caps into thin strips.

In a large saucepot, melt the butter and add the onion, celery, and carrots. Sauté over medium heat until the vegetables are just tender, about 5 minutes. Add the mushrooms and cook about 5 minutes longer, stirring occasionally. Reduce the heat to low and add the flour, stirring well to blend. Continue cooking for 10 to 15 minutes, stirring constantly; if too thick, add a little stock to thin. Slowly stir in the chicken stock and beer and simmer, uncovered, 15 to 20 minutes, stirring occasionally over low heat. Gradually add the cheese, one fourth at a time, whisking well after each addition until melted. Stir in the cream and the cooked rice. Add the salt, Worcestershire, white pepper, and Tabasco and cook a minute. Ladle into bowls and sprinkle with chives.

If Kirin® beer is not available, see Substitution Chart.

SMOKY, SPICY TORTILLA SOUP

6 SERVINGS

*Tortillas can be stacked, rolled, folded, cut, torn, ground, or crumbled.
In this case, corn tortillas not only add special flavor but,
when pureed, give the soup body as well.*

4	tablespoons peanut oil
1	medium onion, *diced*
4	medium cloves garlic, *minced*
4	(6-inch) corn tortillas, *coarsely chopped*
1	canned chipotle chile in adobo sauce
1	tablespoon ground cumin
1/2	cup Rhino Chasers® American Amber Ale
5	large tomatoes, *chopped (about 3 pounds)*
1	small bunch cilantro, *stems removed*
1	quart chicken stock or broth
	Salt and freshly ground pepper, to taste
	Shredded, cooked chicken breast, crisp-fried tortilla strips,
	sour cream, and/or cilantro sprigs, for garnish

In a large saucepot, heat the oil over medium heat. Sauté the onion and garlic just until tender, about 5 minutes. Add the tortillas and sauté until soft, about 3 minutes. Stir in the chipotle chile and cumin and cook 1 minute longer. Stir in the ale and loosen any brown bits at the bottom of the saucepot. Add the tomatoes and cilantro and cook, stirring occasionally, until the tomatoes release their juices, about 10 minutes. Add the chicken broth and bring to a boil. Reduce the heat to a simmer and cook, uncovered, 20 to 30 minutes. Let the soup cool slightly. In a blender or food processor, puree it in several batches. Return the soup to the saucepot and reheat. Season with salt and pepper to taste. Ladle into serving bowls and garnish with shredded chicken, tortilla strips, sour cream, and/or cilantro, as desired.

If Rhino Chasers® American Amber Ale is not available, see Substitution Chart.

ONION PORTER SOUP

8 SERVINGS

Smoky porter has a flavor reminiscent of coffee. Serve this classic in the traditional manner, ladled over toasted croutons and topped with generous amounts of shaved or grated Parmesan cheese.

4	large onions
½	cup butter
2	tablespoons sugar
1	tablespoon chopped fresh thyme leaves
1	(12-ounce) bottle Anchor® Porter
¼	cup dry white wine (optional)
3	cups chicken stock or broth
3	cups beef stock or broth
1	tablespoon kosher salt
1	teaspoon freshly ground pepper
	Toasted croutons
	Freshly grated Parmesan cheese, for garnish

Peel the onions and cut about ½ inch off the stem and root ends. Cut each in half lengthwise. Laying cut side down, cut the onion halves crosswise into thin slices resembling crescent moons. In a large saucepot, melt the butter over medium heat until sizzling. Add the onions and cook, stirring occasionally, until slightly softened, about 6 to 8 minutes. Add the sugar and thyme; cook, stirring often, until the onions begin to brown and caramelize, about 15 to 20 minutes. Pour in the porter and wine and scrape the pan's bottom to loosen any browned bits. Add the chicken and beef stocks, salt and pepper, and bring to a boil. Reduce to a simmer and cook, covered, 1 hour. Occasionally skim and discard any foam that rises to the top. Serve hot, over toasted croutons and garnish with grated Parmesan cheese.

If Anchor® Porter is not available, see Substitution Chart.

PIKE PLACE PALE ALE
MUSSEL BISQUE

4 SERVINGS

Fresh, plump mussels, surrounded by a sea of crimson broth,
make this dish a favorite.

CHEF
MELISSA FLYNN

MERCHANT DU VIN
CORPORATION
SEATTLE, WA

2	bunches scallions, *chopped*
4	medium carrots, *peeled and diced*
2	medium red bell peppers, *cored, seeded, and chopped*
6	small cloves garlic, *minced*
3 to 4	tablespoons olive oil
1	(12-ounce) bottle Pike Place® Pale Ale
2	pounds mussels, *scrubbed, debearded, and rinsed well*
4	tablespoons butter
4	tablespoons all-purpose flour
2	tablespoons canned tomato paste
3	cups milk
1	tablespoon Old Bay seasoning
2	teaspoons hot Hungarian paprika
3	tablespoons chopped fresh Italian parsley, for garnish

In a large saucepot over medium-low heat, sauté the scallions, carrots, red peppers, and garlic in the olive oil until just tender. Add 1 cup of the ale, cover, and simmer 5 minutes. Add the mussels and bring the liquid to a boil. Cover the pot and cook over medium heat until the mussels open, about 5 to 7 minutes. With a slotted spoon, remove and set aside the mussels, discarding any unopened shells. Strain and reserve the broth, discarding the vegetable mixture.

In the same pan, over medium-low heat, heat the butter until bubbly. Add the flour and cook, stirring, until the mixture is foamy. Add the tomato paste and the reserved broth, whisking well. Whisk in the milk, the remaining ½ cup of ale, the Old Bay seasoning, and paprika. While the bisque is heating, remove the mussels from their shells (discarding the shells). Stir the mussels into the hot bisque and remove from the heat. Ladle into serving bowls and garnish with parsley.

❖

If Pike Place® Pale Ale is not available, see Substitution Chart.

BROOKLYN CLAM CHOWDER

6 TO 8 SERVINGS

Manhattan and New England clam chowders have always had a rivalry. A new contender, Brooklyn clam chowder, is a thinner brew with a hearty portion of diced vegetables and clams in every spoonful.

24	cherrystone or littleneck clams, *scrubbed and rinsed well*
2	(12-ounce) bottles Brooklyn® Lager beer
2	cups water
2 to 3	strips bacon, *thinly sliced crosswise*
1	medium onion, *diced*
1	tablespoon Cajun seasoning
½	cup diced carrots
½	cup diced celery
½	cup diced tomato
1	cup diced boiling potato
1	bay leaf
⅛	teaspoon dried thyme leaves, *crushed*
	Parsley sprigs, for garnish (optional)

Place the clams in a large saucepot. Add the beer and water and bring to a boil. Cover the pot tightly and cook over medium-high heat until the clams open, about 5 minutes. Discard any unopened clams.

Meanwhile, in a second large saucepot, over medium heat, cook the bacon until almost crisp, stirring occasionally. Add the onion and Cajun seasoning and sauté until the onion is soft. Add the carrots, celery, and tomato; sauté 2 minutes longer.

Remove the clams from the liquid and set them aside to cool. Allow the liquid to stand 2 to 3 minutes to let the sediment settle to the bottom. Pour the liquid into the pot with the vegetable mixture, being careful to keep the sediment from mixing with the vegetables. Add the potato, bay leaf, and thyme and bring to a boil. Reduce heat to medium-low and cook, uncovered, until the potato is tender, about 15 to 20 minutes.

While the soup is simmering, remove the clams from their shells (discarding the shells) and coarsely chop. When the potato is tender, add the chopped clams and remove the chowder from the heat. Ladle into serving bowls and garnish with sprigs of parsley, if desired.

If Brooklyn® Lager beer is not available, see Substitution Chart.

Note:
When making a cowder, use hard shell clams such as cherrystones or littlenecks with a shell diameter of less than 2 inches for a full-flavored stock.

QUICK WINTER MINESTRONE

8 SERVINGS

JEANNE JONES

COOKBOOK AUTHOR
AND
FOOD CONSULTANT
LA JOLLA, CA

Italian minestrone soup can vary from season to season and region to region, depending on the freshness of the vegetables available. Celis® White beer gives this winter version a light lift without any extra calories; one 8-ounce serving contains only 120 total calories.

2	cups beef, chicken, or vegetable stock or broth
1	(15-ounce) can tomatoes, *undrained and chopped*
¾	cup Celis® White beer
½	medium onion, *chopped*
1	small carrot, *peeled and sliced*
1	celery rib, *chopped*
½	cup chopped white cabbage
¾	teaspoon dried rosemary leaves, *crushed*
¾	teaspoon chili powder
¼	teaspoon salt (omit if using a salted stock)
⅛	teaspoon freshly ground pepper
1	medium clove garlic, *minced*
1	cup undrained canned kidney beans
½	cup cut-up green beans (cut into 1-inch pieces)
½	cup broken-up dry spaghettini (broken into 1-inch pieces)
½	cup freshly grated Parmesan cheese

In a large saucepot, combine the stock, tomatoes, beer, onion, carrot, celery, cabbage, rosemary, chili powder, salt, pepper, and garlic. Bring to a boil: Reduce the heat to a simmer and cook, covered, 30 minutes. Return to a boil; add the kidney and green beans and cook 5 to 10 minutes longer. Add the pasta and continue cooking until al dente, 5 to 6 minutes. Sprinkle in the Parmesan cheese and heat just until the cheese is melted, stirring constantly. Serve hot.

If Celis® White beer is not available, see Substitution Chart.

THAI CLAMS

4 SERVINGS

The Thai curry sauce can be made in advance and reheated. Just add the clams right before serving. All the special ingredients can be found in Asian markets, and the sauce can be easily doubled for larger gatherings.

2 ½	pounds Manila clams
1	tablespoon vegetable oil
½	onion, *thinly sliced*
¼	cup Ballard® Bitter Indian Ale
1	tablespoon yellow curry paste
½	stalk lemongrass, *halved lengthwise (see Note)*
1	(⅛-inch) slice fresh ginger, *slightly mashed*
2	kaffir lime leaves *(see Note)*, or grated zest of 1 lime
1	teaspoon Thai fish sauce
7	ounces coconut milk
¼	cup heavy cream
	Cilantro leaves, for garnish

Scrub, rinse, and dry the clams and set them aside in a covered bowl in the refrigerator.

Heat the oil in a large saucepan over medium-high heat. Sauté the onion until translucent, about 5 minutes. Stir in the ale, reduce the heat, and simmer 3 to 4 minutes. Add the curry paste, turn the heat to medium, and cook, stirring frequently, 1 minute longer. Add the lemongrass, ginger, lime leaves or zest, and the fish sauce, and cook 2 minutes longer. Stir in the coconut milk and cream. Simmer, stirring occasionally, 20 minutes.

Just before serving, add the clams. Cover the pot and cook, stirring occasionally, until the shells open. Remove and discard any unopened clams, the lemongrass, ginger, and lime leaves. Divide clams into serving bowls and top with the sauce. Garnish with cilantro and serve.

If Ballard® Bitter Indian Ale is not available, see Substitution Chart.

KUMAMOTO OYSTERS IN THE HALF SHELL
WITH BOHEMIA BEER MIGNONETTE

4 SERVINGS

The Kumamoto is a Pacific or Japanese oyster.
Oysters from Washington State—Skookum Inlet—are a good substitute.

24	Kumamoto or other Pacific oysters, *rinsed well*
1	cup Bohemia® beer
¼	cup Japanese rice vinegar
4	scallions, *finely chopped*
1	medium tomato, *peeled, seeded, and finely chopped*
½	cup finely chopped cilantro leaves, plus additional whole leaves, for garnish (optional)
1	serrano chile, *seeded and finely chopped*
	Salt and freshly ground pepper, to taste
	Cilantro leaves, for garnish

Open the oysters from the hinged-side with an oyster knife, protecting the hand holding the oyster with a thick towel or heavy glove. Loosen the muscle of each from the top and bottom shell and discard the top shells. Cover and briefly refrigerate the oysters until serving. Combine the remaining ingredients in a medium bowl and chill briefly.

To serve, arrange the oyster halves on a platter of crushed ice. Pour the sauce into a small serving bowl and place in the center of the platter. Garnish with fresh cilantro leaves, if desired.

If Bohemia® beer is not available, see Substitution Chart.

LIME AND SCALLOP CEVICHE

4 TO 6 SERVINGS

In this stimulating combination of color and texture, the flavor of fresh seafood can be highlighted by a crisp, sweet salad.

1	cup Perry's Majestic® Lager beer
1	cup freshly squeezed lime juice
1	cup peeled and diced jicama
1	medium red bell pepper, *cored, seeded, and diced*
1	medium red onion, *diced*
½	medium cucumber, *peeled and diced*
2	tablespoons Chinese hot chili oil
1	tablespoon sugar
1	pound raw bay scallops
	Radicchio lettuce leaves (optional)

In a large bowl, combine all the ingredients except the scallops and radicchio and mix thoroughly. Cover and refrigerate no longer than ½ hour. Two hours before serving, add the scallops. Cover and marinate in the refrigerator for 2 hours. Serve in radicchio lettuce cups, if desired.

If Perry's Majestic® Lager beer is not available, see Substitution Chart.

Note:
If you like your shellfish a little more opaque, marinate the scallops longer.

SHRIMP IN SPICY BATTER

CHEF
JOHN SOLA

DAILY GRILL
LOS ANGELES, CA

A batter that is spicy without overpowering the delicate taste of the shrimp. Serve with lemon wedges, your favorite seafood cocktail sauce, or a spicy tartar sauce.

1	cup cornstarch
½	cup all-purpose flour
½	teaspoon cayenne pepper
½	cup Rhino Chasers® American Amber Ale
2	eggs, *lightly beaten*
1	tablespoon chili paste with garlic *(see Note, page 49)*
	Vegetable oil, for deep frying (about 2 quarts)
2 ½	pounds raw rock shrimp, *peeled and deveined with tails intact*

In a large bowl, stir together the cornstarch, flour, and cayenne pepper. Add the ale, eggs, and chili paste; whisk together well. In a deep-fryer, heat the oil to 375°F. Dip a few of the shrimp at a time into the batter, then carefully slip into the heated oil. Fry 2 to 3 minutes, or until crispy and lightly brown.

With a slotted spoon, remove the shrimp, drain on paper towels and serve.

If Rhino Chasers® American Amber Ale is not available, see Substitution Chart.

CHEF
NOBU MATSUHISA

MATSUHISA
BEVERLY HILLS, CA

NOBU
NEW YORK, NY

EXOTIC GRILLED SPICY SHRIMP

4 APPETIZER SERVINGS

Combining the hot flavors of Asian and Cajun cuisines adds a new kick to sweet tiger shrimp. A glass of refreshing lager will be a welcome chaser to this lively dish.

¾	cup Rhino Chasers® Lager beer
3 to 4	tablespoons Cajun seasoning
1	tablespoon black bean garlic sauce *(see Note)*
1	teaspoon garlic puree
1	teaspoon chili paste with garlic *(see Note)*
2	tablespoons butter
1	pound extra-large, raw tiger shrimp, *peeled and deveined with tails intact*

Preheat a grill or broiler. In a small saucepan, combine the beer, Cajun seasoning, black bean sauce, garlic, and chili paste. Briskly cook over medium-low heat until the sauce thickens, about 8 to 10 minutes. Add the butter and heat just to melt, stirring frequently to keep the butter from separating. Dip the shrimp into the sauce and grill or broil 2 to 3 minutes each side, or until tender.

If Rhino Chasers® Lager beer is not available, see Substitution Chart.

Note:
Thread the shrimp (4 each) onto metal skewers for easier handling. Black bean garlic sauce and chili paste with garlic can be found in Asian markets or in the international food section of some supermarkets.

BASS ALE BATTERED SHRIMP WITH SOY−GINGER DIPPING SAUCE

6 TO 10 SERVINGS

These crisp shrimp are irresistible when dipped in the zesty soy-ginger sauce.

CHEF
MICHAEL McCARTY

MICHAEL'S
RESTAURANT
SANTA MONICA, CA
AND
NEW YORK, NY

1	(12-ounce) bottle Bass® Ale
1 ¼	cups all-purpose flour
3	pounds jumbo shrimp, *peeled and deveined with tails intact*
1	cup soy sauce
3	scallions, *finely chopped*
2	tablespoons sugar
2	tablespoons champagne vinegar
1	tablespoon peeled and finely grated fresh ginger
	Vegetable oil, for deep frying (about 2 quarts)

In a large bowl, whisk together the ale and flour. Cover with plastic wrap and let sit at room temperature 1 hour or longer. Butterfly the shrimp by running a small, sharp knife along the back of each one, cutting almost, but not through to the other side. Flatten the shrimp to open and place on wax paper. Cover and refrigerate until ready to fry.

Meanwhile, to prepare the dipping sauce, combine all the remaining ingredients except the oil. Let stand 30 minutes to blend the flavors.

In a deep-fryer, heat the oil to 375°F. Holding the shrimp by the tail, dip a few at a time into the batter, then carefully slip them into the heated oil. Cook 2 to 3 minutes, or until crisp and golden brown. Remove with a slotted spoon and drain on paper towels. Keep warm while frying the remaining shrimp. Serve immediately, with the dipping sauce.

If Bass® Ale is not available, see Substitution Chart.

SHIITAKE-MUSHROOM-CRUSTED SCALLOPS WITH DARK LAGER—MUSHROOM SYRUP

8 SERVINGS

To further highlight the unique flavor of the mushrooms, scallops are arranged over a delectable shiitake lager syrup.

2	pounds jumbo sea scallops, *rinsed and patted dry*
1	cup Mushroom Flour (see below)
2	tablespoons olive oil
2	tablespoons clarified butter
	Salt and freshly ground white pepper, to taste
1	cup Dark Lager-Mushroom Syrup (see below)
¼	cup sliced chives

Preheat the oven to low. Remove the muscle from each scallop, if attached. Roll the scallops in the mushroom flour to coat lightly. In a large skillet, heat the olive oil and clarified butter over medium-high heat. In two batches, sauté the scallops until lightly brown on both sides and just cooked through, about 3 to 4 minutes. Season with salt and pepper to taste and keep warm in low oven. To serve, spoon about 2 tablespoons of the dark lager—mushroom syrup onto eight small appetizer plates. Divide the scallops and arrange them on top of the syrup. Sprinkle with the chives.

MUSHROOM FLOUR – Makes ½ cup

Place 2 cups (about 15) dried shiitake mushroom caps in a food processor. Process until a fine powder is obtained. Sift through a fine sieve. Reprocess and resift any mushroom pieces, if necessary.

DARK LAGER—MUSHROOM SYRUP – Makes 1 cup

2	cups dried shiitake mushrooms *(see Note)*

Note:
When choosing mushrooms, look for plump ones with the edges curled under. Avoid broken or shriveled caps.

1	quart water
1	(12-ounce) bottle Rhino Chasers® Dark Roasted Läger beer
½	cup sugar

In a large saucepan, combine the dried shiitake mushrooms and the water. Bring to a boil; reduce the heat to a simmer, and gently boil to reduce the liquid to about ½ cup. Strain and reserve the liquid. (The mushrooms can be stored in a sealed container, sliced, and later used in stir-fried dishes.)

Meanwhile, in a small saucepan, combine the lager and sugar. Bring to a boil, stirring to dissolve the sugar. Reduce the heat and gently boil over medium heat to reduce the liquid by half, about 10 minutes. Add the mushroom liquid and continue cooking to reduce to 1 cup. Strain and reheat before serving.

If Rhino Chasers® Dark Roasted Läger beer is not available, see Substitution Chart.

CHEF
MICHAEL S. SHAFER

DEPOT
AN URBAN GRILL
ROOM & BAR
TORRANCE, CA

SHRIMP, SCALLOPS, AND CHICKEN THAI DUMPLINGS

6 SERVINGS

Amber ale and hoisin sauce create a wonderful mahogany steaming sauce for these tasty dumplings.

FILLING

¼	pound peeled, raw rock shrimp or other shrimp, *coarsely chopped*
¼	pound bay scallops, *coarsely chopped*
¼	pound chicken breast, *coarsely chopped*
1	cup soft white bread crumbs
¼	cup minced fresh shiitake mushroom caps
3	tablespoons hoisin or Thai barbecue sauce
1	egg, *lightly beaten*
2	tablespoons minced green onion
1	teaspoon minced pickled ginger
36	wonton skins
	Cornstarch, for dusting
	Green onions, *thinly sliced*, for garnish
	Toasted sesame seeds, for garnish

In a large bowl thoroughly combine all of the filling ingredients. Holding a wonton skin in the palm of your hand, spoon 1 teaspoon of filling into the center. Moisten the edges with water. Fold the skin in half to form a rectangle and gently press the edges to seal. Dabbing water on one corner along the folded edge, bend wonton wrapper to meet the opposite corner. Press to seal with one corner overlapping the other to form a nurse's cap.

Place on wax paper that has been lightly dusted with cornstarch and refrigerate until ready to steam.

STEAMING SAUCE

1	cup Red Tail® Amber Ale
1	cup chicken stock
2	tablespoons hoisin or Thai barbecue sauce
	Sesame oil
2	tablespoons butter

Combine the ale, chicken stock, and hoisin or barbecue sauce and set aside. Heat two large, nonstick skillets (or fry in one skillet, in two batches). Add just enough sesame oil to coat the bottom of each skillet. Add the dumplings and cook over medium-high heat until bottoms are golden-brown, about 2 to 3 minutes. Add half of the ale mixture to each skillet and bring to a boil. Reduce the heat to medium, cover, and cook for 3 to 4 minutes, or until the dumplings are cooked through. Add 1 tablespoon of butter to each skillet and shake gently to melt. Divide evenly and garnish with the green onions and toasted sesame seeds.

❖

If Red Tail® Ale is not available, see Substitution Chart.

CARAMELIZED ONION TART WITH
RED ALE AND SALMON

2 SERVINGS

This recipe has been a signature dish at Pinot Bistro. The preparation time has been simplified, but the presentation still looks as if you've spent hours in the kitchen.

2	tablespoons unsalted butter
I	large red onion, *thinly sliced*
I	fennel bulb, *trimmed and thinly sliced*
I	(12-ounce) bottle Rhino Chasers American Amber Ale
	Salt and freshly ground pepper, to taste
I	sheet puff pastry, *fresh or frozen and defrosted (see Note)*
I	egg, *beaten*
⅓	cup crème fraîche or sour cream
	Cayenne pepper, to taste
	Juice of ½ lemon (about 1½ tablespoons)
3	ounces sliced smoked salmon
½	bunch chives, *chopped*

Melt the butter over medium to low heat in a large skillet. Cook the onion and fennel until soft and caramelized, about 15 minutes. Pour in the ale and gently boil until the ale is nearly evaporated. Season with salt and pepper and set aside.

Preheat the oven to 350°F. Line a baking sheet with parchment paper. With a cookie cutter or a glass, cut the puff pastry into 3-inch-wide circles and transfer to the prepared baking sheet. Brush with beaten egg. Cover the first pan with another baking pan, upside down, to prevent the dough from rising too high. Bake 30 minutes. Transfer to serving plates.

In small bowl, stir together the crème fraîche or sour cream, the cayenne, lemon juice, and salt and pepper to taste.

Divide the onion mixture evenly and place it on top of the pastry. Top each serving with salmon slices and spoon on the crème fraîche. Sprinkle with chives and serve.

If Rhino Chasers American Amber Ale is not available, see Substitution Chart.

Note:
Puff pastry is available in the frozen dessert section at the supermarket. Just follow directions on the package to defrost.

STARTERS

LAGER-CURED SALMON WITH
PORTER AND DIJON FAUX AIOLI

12 APPETIZER OR 6 ENTREE SERVINGS

CHEF

MICHAEL S. SHAFER

DEPOT

AN URBAN GRILL

ROOM & BAR

TORRANCE, CA

This cured salmon can be presented in several ways: as a salad, thinly sliced and served over mixed baby greens with Porter and Dijon Faux Aioli; as a salmon tartare appetizer, coarsely chopped and mixed with shallots, capers, cucumber, and Dijon mustard; or as an entree, thickly sliced and pan-seared. The aioli, or garlic sauce, is also versatile. It is an excellent accompaniment to grilled seafood, poultry, or meat and makes a flavorful dipping sauce for crisp onion rings or grilled vegetables.

1	(1 ½-pound) salmon fillet with skin
¾	cup Rhino Chasers® Lager beer
1	tablespoon minced garlic
¼	cup chopped fresh dill
¼	cup chopped parsley
1 ½	tablespoons coarsely ground pepper
1 ½	tablespoons kosher salt
1 ½	tablespoons sugar
	Lemon slices, for garnish (optional)
	Porter and Dijon Faux Aioli (see below)

Place the salmon fillet, skin-side down, in a glass baking dish just large enough to hold it. Pour the beer over the salmon. Sprinkle the remaining ingredients, except the lemon slices, over the salmon in the above order to form a crust. Cover and marinate in the refrigerator 24 hours. To serve, thinly slice the salmon. Garnish with lemon slices, if desired, and accompany with aioli sauce.

PORTER AND DIJON FAUX AIOLI - Makes about 2 cups

2	cups Anchor® Porter
1	cup rice vinegar
3	medium cloves garlic, *minced*
1	small shallot, *chopped*
1	cup mayonnaise

4	tablespoons Dijon mustard
1	teaspoon dried red pepper flakes
	Salt, to taste

In a large skillet, combine the porter, vinegar, garlic, and shallot. Bring to a boil. Reduce the heat to medium and cook until the liquid is reduced by two thirds, about 5 to 8 minutes. Strain and discard the solids. Cool the remaining liquid. Whisk together the mayonnaise, mustard, red pepper, salt, and the cooled liquid. Serve chilled or at room temperature. The unused portion will keep in the refrigerator in a clean, covered jar for about a week.

❖

If Rhino Chasers® Lager beer and Anchor® Porter is not available, see Substitution Chart.

WELSH RAREBIT

6 SERVINGS

The old farmhouse favorite is transformed into a lighter-than-air cheese soufflé on a chipotle saucer.

CHEF
ROSEMARY HOWE

BARRAUD
CATERERS LTD.
NEW YORK, NY

SAUCERS

4	tablespoons butter
½	teaspoon chipotle chile in adobo sauce, *diced*
⅛	teaspoon salt
6	(3-inch-round, ½-inch-thick) slices challah or brioche
1	teaspoon cooking oil

Preheat the oven to 250°F. Oil six (2-inch) round baking rings with bottoms. Combine the butter, chipotle, and salt in blender and puree. Spread on the bread slices. Place the bread in the oiled rings to form gently sloping saucers. Arrange on baking sheet. Bake until golden brown, 5 minutes. Cool, and then remove the rings, leaving the saucers on the baking sheet.

SOUFFLÉ

2	tablespoons butter
2½	tablespoons flour
¾	cup Samuel Smith® Oatmeal Stout, at room temperature
3	egg yolks
½	cup grated Cheddar cheese
¼	cup crumbled Cheshire cheese
4	egg whites

Preheat the oven to 375°F. Melt the butter in a small saucepan over low heat. Stir in the flour and cook 2 minutes, stirring frequently. Gradually whisk in the beer and cook, stirring constantly, until thickened, about 2 minutes. Remove from the heat and stir in the egg yolks, one at a time. Stir in the cheeses until well blended.

In a dry, clean bowl, whisk the egg whites until stiff peaks form. Add ⅓ of the egg whites to the yolk mixture and gently fold in. Fold in the remaining whites until they just disappear. Mound the filling into the chipotle saucers and bake 10 minutes, until risen and golden brown. Serve immediately.

If Samuel Smith® Oatmeal Stout is not available, see Substitution Chart.

Note:
For an easier
version, the soufflé
can be made in
buttered ramekins
and served with
warm bread and
the chipotle butter.

STARTERS
58

GRILLED RED TAIL CHICKEN BREAST SALAD WITH SALSA VINAIGRETTE

4 SERVINGS

CHEF
JANICE FRANKS

MENDOCINO
BREWING COMPANY
HOPLAND, CA

Adding ale to both the chicken and the salsa makes for a delicious warm salad for a summer evening. Serve it with a hearty loaf of bread and a glass of ale.

GRILLED CHICKEN

½	cup Red Tail® Ale
¼	cup freshly squeezed lime juice
2	tablespoons vegetable oil
2	medium cloves garlic, *minced*
1 to 2	canned chipotle chiles in adobo sauce, *seeded and chopped*
4	boneless, skinless chicken breast halves

SALAD

6	cups torn, assorted salad greens
½	red onion, *sliced*
1	avocado, *sliced*
½	cup drained cooked or canned black beans
¼	cup freshly grated Monterey Jack cheese
	Salsa Vinaigrette (see below)

In a small bowl, whisk together all the grilled chicken ingredients except the breast halves. Place the chicken breasts in a glass dish just large enough to hold them. Pour the ale mixture over the chicken to coat it evenly. Cover and marinate in the refrigerate 6 hours to overnight.

To cook, preheat the grill. Remove the chicken breasts from the marinade and grill over glowing coals or medium heat 5 to 6 minutes on each side, brushing it occasionally with the marinade. Slice across the width. To serve, arrange a bed of salad greens on four individual serving plates. Top with a sliced chicken breast. Garnish each serving with the red onion, avocado, black beans, and cheese. Spoon the salsa vinaigrette equally over each salad or as desired.

SALSA VINAIGRETTE – Makes 2 ½ cups

3 to 4	large Roma (Italian plum) tomatoes, *chopped* (about 1 ½ cups)
⅔	cup seasoned rice vinegar
¼	cup freshly squeezed lime juice
2 to 3	scallions, *chopped*
2	tablespoons finely chopped cilantro
1	canned chipotle chile in adobo sauce, *seeded and finely chopped*
¼	cup Red Tail® Ale

In a medium bowl, combine all the ingredients except the ale; chill. Stir in the ale just before serving.

If Red Tail® Ale is not available, see Substitution Chart.

TOSSED SALAD WITH WHEAT BEER VINAIGRETTE

4 SERVINGS

Any combination of crisp chilled greens goes well with light Wheat Beer Vinaigrette.

CHEF
JOHN DICKINSON

WYNKOOP
BREWING COMPANY
DENVER, CO

WHEAT BEER VINAIGRETTE – Makes 1 ½ cups

¼	cup Dijon mustard
¼	cup white wine vinegar
½	cup Wynkoop® Wilderness Wheat beer
½	cup canola oil
2	tablespoons minced chives
2	tablespoons minced parsley
2	tablespoons freshly squeezed lemon juice
	Salt and freshly ground pepper, to taste
	Salad (see below)

In the bowl of a food processor, blend the mustard, vinegar, and beer. While the processor is running, slowly dribble the oil into the mixture a few drops at a time. Then pour in a slow, steady stream of oil until it has been incorporated and emulsified. Add the herbs, lemon juice, and salt and pepper. Drizzle over the tossed salad to coat lightly. Gently toss and serve immediately.

SALAD – 4 servings

2	heads Boston lettuce
2	heads Belgian endive
1	cucumber, peeled
½	red onion, *thinly sliced*

Rinse and pat dry the lettuce. Tear the Boston leaves into bite-sized pieces and place in a salad bowl. Stack the endive and cut it crosswise into ½-inch slices; add to the bowl.

Halve the cucumber lengthwise; scrape out and discard the seeds. Cut into ¼-inch slices. Add the cucumber and onion to bowl and toss well. Refrigerate until ready to toss with the dressing (immediately before serving).

If Wynkoop® Wilderness Wheat beer is not available, see Substitution Chart.

CHEECH'S WETBACK
(FOR A LIQUID DIET)

I SERVING

1   lime, quartered

         Tequila

         Salt

1   (12-ounce) bottle Rhino Chasers® Lager beer

No more needs to be said!

Prepare condiments.

Slice lime into wedges (preferably use a machete).

There are many varieties of tequila. I recommend Patron (because I'll get free Patron after this).

Open the bottle and assume a comfortable position.

Warm up wrist—flex once or twice.

Prepare hand—lick clean of any debris…if you don't have a French tongue, a domestic one will do.

Pour salt on left hand—lick it up.

Take bite out of lime wedge.

Pick up tequila in hand with well-warmed-up right wrist.

Down shot of tequila in one gulp.

Scrunch up your face (closest I'll come to an aerobic exercise).

Let out big aaaahhhh (yoga breathing exercise).

Reach for Rhino Chasers® Lager beer with left hand (stretching exercise).

Take a big gulp.

Let out another breath…aaaahhhh.

One big burp before chanting OM MANI PADME OM RHINO O

Gaze fondly at sunset…or sunrise.

Repeat as often as necessary.

A smoking break is recommended.

Serves one to ten comfortably.

If Rhino Chasers® Lager beer is not available, see Substitution Chart.

Note:
Recipe can
be doubled,
tripled, etc.

Seafood

The versatility of beer in the kitchen is demonstrated
once again when we turn to preparing seafood. As compared with meat,
it takes more care to cook fish or shellfish with beer, but the results can be
deliciously rewarding. Beer has a special affinity for crustaceans, as is evident
from many traditional recipes found in Scandinavia, as well as in
Belgium and the Netherlands, in which shrimps and crayfish are
simmered in the local brews.

Used judiciously—without permitting the hops or malt to
overpower the natural flavor of the fish—it can also add a subtle accent
to everything from trout to tuna, and nothing contributes more to the
seductiveness of a fish stew or a chowder than a
dash of ale in the stock.

SAUTÉED GROUPER WITH FRESH PEARS AND APRICOTS

4 SERVINGS

This crisp, fried fish with warm fruit sauce is a wonderful dish for the first autumn get-together.

1	cup Great Lakes® Wit's End beer
2	medium pears, *peeled, cored, and cut into ½-inch cubes*
3	apricots, *pitted and quartered*
½	teaspoon finely chopped fresh thyme leaves
1 to 2	tablespoons butter
4	grouper, sea bass, or halibut fillets (about 6 ounces each)
½	cup all-purpose flour
¼	cup vegetable oil

In a medium saucepan, combine the beer, pears, and apricots. Cook over medium heat, uncovered, until the fruit is tender and the liquid thickens slightly, about 10 minutes. Stir in the thyme and butter just to melt, and remove from the heat.

Meanwhile, dip the fish into the flour and shake off any excess. In a large skillet, heat the oil and sauté the fish until golden brown, about 4 to 5 minutes per side. Serve the sauce over the fish.

If Great Lakes® Wit's End beer is not available, see Substitution Chart.

GINGER WHEAT DEEP-FRIED FISH FILLETS

4 SERVINGS

CHEF
WESLIE EVANS

THE GREAT LOST BEAR
PORTLAND, ME

To make a tasty "fish 'n chips" meal, deep-fry some thickly sliced or thinly wedged potatoes and serve them with the fish.

1 ¼	cups all-purpose flour
2	teaspoons cayenne pepper
1	teaspoon freshly ground white pepper
1	teaspoon paprika
1	teaspoon salt
1	cup Lompoc® Ginger Wheat beer
2	tablespoons coconut milk
2	tablespoons butter, *melted*
2	eggs, *separated*
2	teaspoons minced fresh ginger
	Vegetable oil, for deep frying (about 2 quarts)
8	haddock or cod fillets (about 2 pounds)

In a large bowl, stir together the flour, cayenne, white pepper, paprika, and salt. Add the beer, coconut milk, melted butter, egg yolks, and ginger. Beat with a whisk until well blended. Cover and refrigerate 15 to 30 minutes.

In a deep-fryer, heat the oil to 375°F. With an electric mixer, beat the egg whites until soft peaks form. Gently fold the beaten egg whites into the beer batter. Dip the fish fillets into the batter, a few at a time, then carefully slip them into the heated oil. Cook until golden brown, then turn with tongs to brown the second side, about 3 to 5 minutes total. Remove the fried fillets and drain them on paper towels. Keep warm while preparing the remaining fish.

If Lompoc® Ginger Wheat beer is not available, see Substitution Chart.

*Note:
For a little more "heat," serve the fried fillets with bottled Thai chili sauce.*

CHEF
MARIE-CLAIRE
QUITTELIER

❧

BELGIAN TRADING
COMPANY
AUSTIN, TX

HALIBUT WITH SHALLOTS AND WHITE BEER

6 SERVINGS

Whatever firm-fleshed fish steaks (swordfish, salmon, Chilean sea bass, etc.) are on special in the market can be substituted for the halibut in this easy baked entree.

10	medium shallots, *minced*
1 ½	tablespoons butter
¾	cup Celis® White beer
	Salt and freshly ground pepper, to taste
6	halibut steaks (1 to 1 ¼ inches thick)
6	lemon slices
2	tablespoons heavy cream
2	tablespoons finely chopped fresh Italian parsley

Preheat the oven to 425°F. In a medium skillet, sauté the shallots in 1 tablespoon of the butter until just tender, about 5 minutes. Stir in 2 tablespoons of the beer and set aside. Butter an ovenproof baking dish large enough to hold the halibut with the remaining ½ tablespoon of butter. Spoon the cooked shallots evenly over the bottom of the dish. Salt and pepper the halibut on both sides and arrange the fish in a single layer over the shallots. Place a slice of lemon on each steak. In the same skillet, bring the remaining beer to a boil and stir in the cream. Pour over the fish. Bake 10 to 15 minutes, until the fish tests done *(see Note)*. To serve, transfer the halibut to a serving platter; top with the shallots, and sprinkle with the parsley.

If Celis® White beer is not available, see Substitution Chart.

Note:
To check for doneness, with a fork, loosen the flesh around the bone. If it is milk-white in color, the fish is fully cooked. If the flesh is still transparent, bake a few minutes longer.

POACHED SALMON IN WHEAT BEER BROTH WITH SUMMER TOMATO SALAD

4 SERVINGS

Here is an elegant cold entree for summer entertaining.

	Olive oil, for coating
4	(7-ounce) salmon fillets
4	cups Redhook® Wheat beer
	Juice of 1 lemon (about 3 tablespoons)
	Juice of 1 orange (about 6 tablespoons)
	Juice of 1 lime (about 2 tablespoons)
½	onion, *sliced*
1	stalk lemongrass
	Salt and freshly ground pepper, to taste
1	bunch opal basil stems
	Summer Tomato Salad (see below)

Coat a large sauté pan with oil and arrange the salmon fillets in a single layer. Add the remaining ingredients (except the salad), cover with a lid or parchment paper, and bring to a simmer over medium heat. Simmer 6 to 8 minutes. Remove from the heat and cool in the liquid.

To serve, divide the tomato salad and arrange it on four serving plates. Place the cold salmon over (or alongside) the salad. Garnish with the reserved citrus sections.

SUMMER TOMATO SALAD – Makes 5 cups

4	plum tomatoes, *quartered*
2 to 3	beefsteak tomatoes, *halved*
1	pint cherry tomatoes, *stemmed and halved*
1	pint yellow pear tomatoes, *stemmed and halved*
1	bunch opal basil leaves, *chopped*
2	medium lemons
2	medium oranges
2	medium limes
½	cup extra-virgin olive oil
	Salt and freshly ground pepper, to taste

Combine all the tomatoes and the basil in large bowl. Working over a bowl to catch the juices, section and peel the lemons, oranges, and limes. Set aside and reserve half the fruit for garnish and put the rest in the bowl. Add the olive oil to the juices and fruit in the bowl, season with salt and pepper and whisk to combine. Pour the dressing over the tomato salad and toss gently to combine.

If Redhook® Wheat beer is not available, see Substitution Chart.

RED SNAPPER IN BEER
VINEGAR SAUCE

6 SERVINGS

This colorful, flavorful sauce goes equally well with cod fillets.

1 ½	cups Pyramid® Wheat beer
2	large tomatoes, *peeled, seeded, and pureed (see Note)*
¼	cup apple cider vinegar
2	tablespoons minced shallots
6	red snapper fillets (about 2 pounds)
	Salt and freshly ground pepper, to taste
¼	cup heavy cream
2	tablespoons drained capers

In a large nonstick skillet, combine the beer, tomato puree, vinegar, and shallots. Bring to a boil over high heat. Reduce the heat to medium and cook, stirring occasionally, until most of the liquid has evaporated, about 7 to 10 minutes. Place the fish fillets on top of the tomato mixture and sprinkle with the salt and pepper. Cover and simmer for about 7 minutes, or until the fish is just done. Transfer the fish to a serving platter and keep warm. Add the cream to the tomato mixture and boil gently to thicken slightly. Stir in the capers, and season with salt and pepper to taste. Spoon the sauce over the fish to serve.

If Pyramid® Wheat beer is not available, see Substitution Chart.

CHEF
ANN WALKER

ANN WALKER
CATERING, INC.
CORTE MADERA, CA

Note:
An easy way to puree the tomatoes is to cut each tomato in half crosswise. Gently squeeze each half to remove the seeds. Then grate each half on a box-type grater over a bowl until all you have in your hand is the tomato skin, and in the bowl, the peeled, seeded, and pureed tomatoes.

CHEF
BILLY HAHN

HARBORSIDE
RESTAURANT/
McCORMICK &
SCHMICK
PORTLAND, OR

APRICOT ALE—GLAZED SALMON

2 SERVINGS

Complete this delicious entree for two with rice pilaf
and steamed fresh asparagus.

1	tablespoon olive oil
1	salmon fillet (about 12 ounces)
8	dried apricot halves, *diced*
¼	cup Rhino Chasers® Peach Honey Wheat beer
1	tablespoon freshly squeezed lemon juice
2	tablespoons butter
	Sliced chives, for garnish

Preheat the oven to low. In a large skillet, heat the olive oil over medium-high heat. Sear the salmon on one side; turn and reduce the heat to low. Add the apricots, beer, and lemon juice. Cover and simmer for 8 to 10 minutes, or until the fish is done. Transfer the salmon to a serving platter and keep warm in a low oven.

Increase the heat and reduce the liquid in the skillet to about 1 tablespoon. Lower the heat and stir in the butter until smooth. Spoon the sauce over the salmon and sprinkle with the chives.

If Rhino Chasers® Peach Honey Wheat beer is not available, see Substitution Chart.

BROILED SALMON WITH
BARBECUE BEER GLAZE

4 SERVINGS

*Reducing or boiling down the ingredients intensifies the
flavors of this barbecue-style beer glaze.*

2	cups Rhino Chasers® Dark Roasted Läger beer
¼	cup brown sugar
¼	cup Dijon mustard
¼	cup white wine vinegar
4	teaspoons Worcestershire sauce
½	teaspoon freshly ground pepper
4	salmon steaks or fillets (6 to 7 ounces each)
	Lemon wedges, for garnish

To make the glaze, in a medium saucepan, combine the beer, brown sugar, mustard, vinegar,
Worcestershire sauce, and pepper. Cook over medium heat, stirring occasionally, until the
liquid is reduced by half and has the consistency of honey, about 7 minutes. Pour into a
glass bowl. Place the bowl into an ice bath and chill, stirring occasionally, or refrigerate.

Preheat the broiler. Arrange the salmon in one layer in a large glass dish. Spoon
the cooled glaze over both sides of the fish and marinate 15 minutes. Place the salmon on
a broiler pan and broil 6 inches from the heat for 4 to 5 minutes per side, basting once or
twice with any remaining glaze. Serve with lemon wedges.

If Rhino Chasers® Dark Roasted Läger beer is not available, see Substitution Chart.

*Note:
The salmon can
also be barbecued
on a grill 6 inches
above the coals,
or over medium
heat on a
gas barbecue.*

BONELESS TROUT WITH BELGIAN ALE

4 SERVINGS

Baking the trout is easy, and a flavorful change from the usual pan-fried presentation.

3	tablespoons butter
2	medium leeks, *well rinsed and cut into 2-inch julienne strips*
2	carrots, *cut into 2-inch julienne strips*
1	cup small, button mushrooms, *quartered*
2	medium shallots, *sliced*
4	boneless trout, *rinsed and patted dry* (12 ounces each)
1	(12-ounce) bottle Chimay® Ale *(see Note)*
	Salt and freshly ground pepper, to taste
3	tablespoons heavy cream
	Juice of 1 lemon (about 3 tablespoons)

Preheat the oven to 375°F. In a large skillet, melt the butter and sauté the leeks, carrots, mushrooms, and shallots over medium heat for 2 to 3 minutes. Transfer the vegetables to a flameproof baking dish large enough to hold the trout. Place the trout over the vegetables and pour the ale over all. Season with salt and pepper to taste. Cover the dish with aluminum foil and bake 15 to 20 minutes, turning the fish once, carefully, halfway through the cooking time, until done and the fish is firm to the touch. Lift out the trout and transfer it to a serving platter. Keep warm in a low oven.

Place the baking pan on a top burner and pour in the cream. Cook over medium-high heat, stirring occasionally, until the liquid is reduced by about one third, or until the sauce is thickened to taste. Add the lemon juice and salt and pepper to taste. Spoon the sauce over the trout and serve.

If Chimay® Ale is not available, see Substitution Chart.

GRILLED WATER PRAWNS AND ROASTED PEPPER VINAIGRETTE

4 SERVINGS

CHEF
LYNNE ARONSON

LOLA
NEW YORK, NY

Serve these beer-marinated shrimps with beer biscuits and ice-cold beer for a truly beery barbecue.

1	tablespoon unsalted butter
1	medium shallot, *chopped*
2	cloves garlic, *chopped*
2	tablespoons brown sugar
4	ounces rice wine vinegar
6	saffron threads
4	cups New Amsterdam® Ale
16	large shrimp, *backs butterflied with shells on*
	Roasted Pepper Beer Vinaigrette (see below)

Melt the butter in a medium saucepan over medium heat. Sauté the shallot and garlic until soft. Stir in the sugar, vinegar, saffron, and ale. Bring to a boil, reduce to a simmer and cook for 10 minutes. Pour into a large bowl and set it aside to cool. When cool, stir in the shrimp. Cover and marinate in the refrigerator for 2 hours. Thread the shrimp on skewers and set aside.

Preheat the grill or barbecue. Grill the shrimp until they are opaque and firm, about 2–3 minutes each side. Serve with roasted pepper beer vinaigrette for dipping.

ROASTED PEPPER BEER VINAIGRETTE

¼	cup rice wine vinegar
2	tablespoons Dijon mustard
¼	cup New Amsterdam® Ale
3	tablespoons honey
1	tablespoon chopped shallot
½	cup roasted red peppers
1	cup extra virgin olive oil
	Salt and freshly ground pepper, to taste

Combine the vinegar, mustard, ale, honey, shallot, and the red peppers in a blender. Puree until smooth. Drizzle in the oil and puree until smooth. Season to taste with salt and pepper.

If New Amsterdam® Ale is not available, see Substitution Chart.

*Note:
These shrimp can be
broiled 5 inches
from the heat,
2–3 minutes each side.*

SHRIMP SAUTÉ WITH RASPBERRY LAMBIC SAUCE

4 SERVINGS

Colorful vegetables accent this garlic-infused shrimp sauté.
We like it over a bed of short grain rice.

SHRIMP AND VEGETABLES

4	tablespoons olive oil
24	extra-large raw shrimp, *peeled and deveined*
1	cup thinly sliced scallions *(cut on the diagonal)*
½	cup julienned red bell pepper
½	cup thinly sliced asparagus spears *(cut on the diagonal)*
½	cup quartered and julienned crookneck or other yellow squash
4	tablespoons minced garlic
2	tablespoons julienned fresh basil leaves
2	tablespoons chopped parsley
	Raspberry Lambic Sauce (see below)

In a large skillet, heat 3 tablespoons of the olive oil over medium heat. Add the shrimp and sauté just until tender, 2 to 3 minutes. With a slotted spoon, remove the shrimp and set aside. Add the remaining 1 tablespoon of oil to the skillet. Sauté the vegetables and herbs over medium heat, stirring often, until the vegetables are just tender, about 3 minutes. Stir the shrimp into the vegetable mixture and remove from the heat. Spoon the sauce over the shrimp and vegetables to serve.

RASPBERRY LAMBIC SAUCE – Makes ¼ cup

½	tablespoon olive oil
2	tablespoons minced shallots
¼	cup Lindemans® Lambic Frambois
½	cup chicken stock or broth
1	tablespoon unsalted butter
	Salt and freshly ground pepper, to taste

In a small skillet, heat the oil over medium heat. Sauté the shallots until lightly browned. Add the beer and cook to reduce the liquid by half, about 2 to 3 minutes. Add the chicken stock and cook to reduce by one fourth. Whisk in the butter until smooth and remove from the heat. Season with salt and pepper to taste.

If Lindemans® Lambic Frambois is not available, see Substitution Chart.

STEAMED SALMON

2 SERVINGS

Complete this meal for two with rice pilaf or mixed grains and fresh green beans. The sauce from the salmon will complement them all.

1	cup Samuel Adams® Triple Bock beer
2	tablespoons finely chopped shallots
1	tablespoon minced garlic
1	sprig fresh thyme
1	bay leaf
2	(1-inch-thick) salmon fillets (6 ounces each)
	Salt and freshly ground pepper, to taste
2	tablespoons unsalted butter

In the bottom of a medium saucepan fitted with a rack or vegetable steamer raised at least 1 inch, combine the beer, shallots, garlic, and herbs. Bring to a boil.

Season the salmon with salt and pepper. Place the fish on the rack, cover, and steam 7 to 10 minutes, or until the fish is opaque and firm when pressed lightly with a finger. Remove the salmon and keep warm (placing a plate over the salmon works well). Remove the rack. Cook the remaining liquid over medium heat until it is reduced to 1 to 2 tablespoons. Whisk in the butter and season with salt and pepper to taste. Strain and serve over the salmon fillets.

If Samuel Adams® Triple Bock beer is not available, see Substitution Chart.

SPICY HONEY BEER–GLAZED SHRIMP

4 SERVINGS

These spicy and sweet shrimp rest on a bed of steamed baby bok choy.

1	cup Perry's Majestic® Lager beer
½	cup toasted sesame seeds
½	cup honey
¼	cup dark soy sauce
¼	cup sesame oil
3	tablespoons hot chili oil
1	pound medium to large raw shrimp, *peeled and deveined*
	Peanut oil, for coating skillet
4	heads baby bok choy, *thinly sliced*

To make the marinade, combine the beer, sesame seeds, honey, soy sauce, sesame oil, and chili oil in a large bowl. Add the shrimp and marinate in the refrigerator for 30 minutes. Preheat oven to low. Drain and reserve the marinade. Lightly coat a large skillet set over medium-high heat with the peanut oil. Sauté the shrimp just until tender, 2 to 3 minutes. Remove the shrimp and keep warm in a low oven. To make the sauce, pour the reserved marinade into the skillet and cook over medium heat, stirring occasionally, until reduced by half, about 10 minutes.

Meanwhile, steam the bok choy in a bamboo or metal steamer over boiling water just until tender, about 4 minutes. To serve, arrange the bok choy on a serving platter, top with the shrimp, and drizzle the sauce over all.

If Perry's Majestic® Lager beer is not available, see Substitution Chart.

SPICY CRAYFISH

*Peeled crayfish, or crawfish, are available frozen at many
supermarket fish counters.*

¼	cup olive oil
1	tablespoon minced garlic
1 ½	cups chopped onions
1	red bell bell pepper, *cored, seeded, and diced*
1	green bell pepper, *cored, seeded, and diced*
½	cup chopped celery
¾	cup Rhino Chasers® American Amber Ale
1	tablespoon all-purpose flour
½	teaspoon dried thyme
½	teaspoon dried oregano
½	teaspoon cayenne pepper
1	teaspoon freshly ground black pepper
1	teaspoon coarse salt
¼	cup chicken stock
1 ½	pounds peeled crayfish tails

Heat 3 tablespoons of the oil in a large skillet over medium heat. Sauté the garlic, onions, peppers, and celery until soft, about 8 minutes. Pour in ¼ cup of the ale and boil 3 minutes. Transfer the vegetables to a platter. Return the skillet to heat.

Heat the remaining tablespoon of oil, sprinkle in the flour, and stir until smooth and golden. Pour in the remaining ale, whisking constantly for about 3 minutes, being careful not to scorch the flour. Add the thyme, oregano, cayenne, black pepper, salt, and the reserved onion mixture and sauté about 2 minutes longer. Pour in the chicken stock and cook another minute. Stir in the crayfish and cook 5 minutes longer. Serve immediately.

If Rhino Chasers® American Amber Ale is not available, see Substitution Chart.

LUCIA'S SPICY SEA SCALLOPS

LUCIA HWONG

COMPOSER
NEW YORK, NY

4 SERVINGS

These delicate sea scallops are accented with complex Pacific Rim flavors and served over a bed of pasta for a substantial seafood entree.

1	teaspoon prepared black bean sauce with chili
1	(12-ounce) bottle plus ¼ cup Rhino Chasers® Lager beer
¼	cup prepared Thai peanut sauce
½	teaspoon salt
2	pounds sea scallops, *rinsed*
3	tablespoons vegetable oil
6	tablespoons finely chopped shallots
1	red bell pepper, *cored, seeded, and chopped*
1	green bell pepper, *cored, seeded, and chopped*
¼	cup all-purpose flour
5	tablespoons sesame oil
1	tablespoon minced fresh ginger
2	tablespoons oyster sauce
2	tablespoons rice vinegar
1	pound penne pasta, *cooked and drained*
2	tablespoons toasted sesame seeds
5	sprigs cilantro, for garnish

Combine the black bean sauce, ¼ cup of the lager, the Thai peanut sauce, and salt in a small bowl and reserve.

Place the scallops in another bowl. Pour in the remaining lager and marinate in the refrigerator for about 10 minutes.

Heat the vegetable oil in a large skillet over high heat. Sauté 3 tablespoons of the shallots for 2 minutes. Stir in the red and green peppers and sauté 5 minutes longer. Stir in 3 tablespoons of the reserved black bean sauce mixture and cook briefly. Transfer to a platter and reserve. Drain the scallops and pat dry. Roll them in the flour to coat evenly and pat off the excess.

Heat 2 tablespoons of the sesame oil in a skillet over medium to high heat and briefly sauté the ginger. Add the remaining shallots and stir-fry briefly. Push the ginger and shallots to the sides of the pan and sauté scallops in the center for about 1 minute on each side. Return the pepper mixture to the pan, stirring gently to combine. Adjust the seasonings with more of the black bean sauce mixture, as desired. Mix together the remaining sesame oil, the oyster sauce, and rice vinegar. Pour over the hot pasta, tossing well to combine. To serve, divide pasta among four warm serving plates. Top with the scallops, sprinkle with sesame seeds, and garnish with cilantro. Serve immediately.

If Rhino Chasers® Lager beer is not available, see Substitution Chart.

SPAGHETTI WITH SCALLOPS AND ALE

4 SERVINGS

CHEF
PINO LUONGO

IL TOSCANACCIO
NEW YORK, NY

*This delicious seafood sauce cooks in the time
it takes to prepare the spaghetti.*

1	pound spaghetti
3	medium cloves garlic, *crushed*
½	cup olive oil
1	pound bay scallops
1	cup Rhino Chasers® American Amber Ale
1	tablespoon fresh thyme leaves

Cook the spaghetti in a large pot of boiling salted water, until al dente. Drain and reserve. In a large skillet, sauté the garlic in the olive oil until golden brown, about 3 minutes. Add the scallops and cook over low heat until the scallops are golden brown and just cooked through, about 3 minutes. With a slotted spoon, remove the scallops and set aside. Remove and discard the garlic. Pour off and reserve the oil. Add the ale to the pan and cook over medium heat to reduce the liquid by half, about 3 to 4 minutes. Add the cooked, drained spaghetti and return the scallops to the skillet. Cook 1 minute longer. Add the thyme and 4 tablespoons of the reserved olive oil. Toss the spaghetti to coat well and cook briefly, about 15 seconds. Serve immediately.

If Rhino Chasers® American Amber Ale is not available, see Substitution Chart.

LINGUINE WITH CLAMS, SHRIMP, AND RED CHILE PESTO

6 SERVINGS

Red chile pesto is a wonderful base for this pasta dish. The extra pesto can be stored, tightly covered, in the refrigerator for 2 weeks. Use it to add zing to your favorite dishes.

1	pound linguine
2	Manila clams, *scrubbed*
2	large shrimp, *peeled and deveined*
2	cups heavy cream
¼	cup Red Chile Pesto (see below)
	Salt and freshly ground pepper, to taste
½	bunch cilantro, stems removed, for garnish

Cook the linguine in a large pot of salted water. While the linguine is cooking, place cream along with the clams and shrimp in a large sauté pan. Cook over high heat until the clams open and the shrimp are cooked, about 10 minutes. Remove the clams and shrimp and set aside in a warm place (discard any unopened clams). Continue to let the cream reduce about 4 minutes longer. Whisk in ¼ cup of the red chile pesto and season with salt and pepper to taste. Drain and rinse the pasta. In a warm bowl, toss pasta, sauce, and shellfish. Garnish with the cilantro.

RED CHILE PESTO - Makes 2 cups

4	dried New Mexico chiles
8	dried chipotle chiles
1	bunch cilantro, *stems removed*
2	cloves garlic, *minced*
1	medium white onion, *diced*
⅓	Anchor® Steam Ale
⅓	cup lime juice
1	cup peanut oil

Soak both types of chiles in hot water until softened, at least 1 hour. Remove the stems and seeds (if your skin is sensitive, wear rubber gloves).

Combine the drained chiles, 1 bunch of the cilantro, the garlic, onion, ale, and lime juice in a food processor fitted with a metal blade. With the motor running, add the peanut oil in a thin, steady stream until emulsified. Set the pesto aside until needed.

If Anchor® Steam Ale is not available, see Substitution Chart.

LOUISIANA BOUILLABAISSE

6 SERVINGS

*Hot and spicy New Orleans bouillabaisse is a perfect match for any beer.
If you can't find salsify, a root vegetable also known as oyster plant,
substitute potatoes and cook 10 minutes longer.*

1	tablespoon Brewhouse Seasoning (see page 90)
1	ounce clarified butter
12	ounces lobster tails, *removed from their shells, cut in large chunks*
1	dozen clams, *scrubbed*
1	dozen mussels, *debearded and scrubbed*
1	dozen large shrimp, *peeled and deveined*
2	tablespoons clarified butter
10	ounces Red Stallion® beer
½	pound tuna fillet, *cut into 4 strips*
½	pound salmon fillet, *cut into 4 strips*
½	cup chopped scallions
1	cup diced onions
1	cup seeded and diced tomatoes
3 ¾	cups fish stock or ½ clam juice and ½ water
4	ribs Swiss chard, *julienned*
2	stalks salsify, *cubed,* or 1 cup cubed potatoes
2	tablespoons fresh lemon juice
4	sprigs fresh rosemary, for garnish
	Lemon wedges, for garnish

Sprinkle the Brewhouse Seasoning evenly over all the seafood. Heat the butter in a large
stockpot over medium heat and sauté the lobsters, clams, and mussels, stirring frequently,
for about 3 minutes. Add the shrimp and sauté until pink.

Pour in the beer and cook over medium-high heat until reduced by half, about
7 minutes. Add the tuna and salmon and cook 2 to 3 minutes longer (discard any unopened
mussels and clams). Add the scallions, onions, and tomatoes, and cook 1 minute longer. Pour
in the fish stock or clam juice and water. Bring to a simmer and cook 3 minutes longer. Stir
in the Swiss chard, salsify and lemon juice and remove from the heat. Ladle into bowls, garnish

with rosemary and lemon wedges and serve.

BREWHOUSE SEASONING – Makes 2 ½ tablespoons

1	teaspoon cayenne pepper
½	teaspoon paprika
3 to 4	teaspoons salt
1	teaspoon freshly ground white pepper
1	teaspoon freshly ground black pepper
1	teaspoon garlic powder

Mix together in a small bowl.

If Red Stallion® beer is not available, see Substitution Chart.

PAELLA

8 SERVINGS

*There is not a paella recipe in existence that has a short ingredients list.
Although this one is no exception, it is guaranteed to be
worth the effort involved.*

½	pound boneless, skinless chicken breast halves, *cut into 1-inch pieces*
	Salt and freshly ground pepper, to taste
¾	cup olive oil
2	pinches saffron threads
½	pound hot Italian turkey sausage, *cut into ½-inch slices*
1	cup Rhino Chasers® American Amber Ale
1	pound large raw shrimp, *peeled and deveined, with tails intact* (reserve shells)
5	tablespoons minced garlic
2	teaspoons chili paste with garlic *(see Note)*
2	tablespoons dry white wine
1	pound littleneck clams, *scrubbed and rinsed well*
2	medium onions, *chopped*
1	cup chopped fresh Italian parsley
1 ½	cups chopped red bell pepper
½	cup finely chopped shallots
1	pound bay scallops
½	cup chopped green bell pepper
4	tablespoons butter
1 ½	cups diced carrots
2	cups chicken stock or broth
1 ½	cups peeled, seeded, and chopped tomatoes
2	cups basmati rice

Season the chicken with the salt and pepper. In a large skillet, heat 2 tablespoons of the olive oil over medium to high heat. Sauté the chicken with a pinch of saffron until lightly browned, about 2 minutes. Transfer to a large bowl and set aside.

To the same skillet, add 1 tablespoon of the oil. Sauté the sausage until lightly browned, about 2 minutes. Add ¼ cup of the ale and cook 3 minutes longer. With a slotted spoon remove the sausage and set aside.

*Note:
Chili paste with
garlic can be found in
Asian markets or in
the international food
section of some
supermarkets.*

Add 2 more tablespoons of the oil and sauté the shrimp and 1 teaspoon of the garlic over medium to high heat just until the shrimp changes color. Add a dash of salt, 1 teaspoon of the chili paste, and the wine; cook 30 seconds longer. Transfer to the bowl with the chicken.

Add 2 more tablespoons of the oil and the clams, ¼ cup of the onions, 1 tablespoon of the garlic, 2 tablespoons of the parsley, 1 tablespoon of the red pepper, and ½ cup of the ale. Bring to a boil over medium to high heat, cover, and cook, gently shaking the skillet occasionally, until the clams open, about 5 minutes. Transfer the clams to the bowl with the chicken, discarding any that haven't opened. Pour the clam liquid remaining in the skillet into a second bowl and reserve.

Add 2 more tablespoons of the oil to the pan and sauté 1 tablespoon of the shallots over medium heat until softened, about 2 minutes. Add the scallops, the remaining teaspoon of chili paste, and a pinch of saffron; sauté 2 minutes longer. Remove the scallops to the bowl with the chicken and pour any liquid in the skillet into the reserved clam liquid.

Sauté the green pepper and the remaining red pepper in 2 tablespoons of the oil until crisp-tender, about 2 minutes. Remove and set aside.

Heat 2 tablespoons of the butter over medium heat and sauté the remaining garlic and shallots 1 to 2 minutes. Add the carrots and the remaining onions. Sauté just until tender, about 4 minutes. Add the remaining ¼ cup of ale and cook 2 minutes longer. Remove the skillet from the heat and set aside.

In a medium saucepan, combine the reserved shrimp shells and 1 cup of water; boil, uncovered, for 5 minutes. Strain the shells and discard. Add the shrimp broth to the clam-scallop liquid. The combined seafood liquid should make about 1 ½ cups.

Add the seafood liquid, chicken stock, and tomatoes to the skillet with the onion-carrot mixture. Bring to a boil. Reduce to a simmer and cook, uncovered, for 5 minutes. Remove from the heat.

In a large saucepot or Dutch oven, heat the remaining 2 tablespoons of butter and 1 tablespoon of oil over medium-high heat. Sauté the rice until lightly browned over medium-high heat, stirring constantly. Add the contents of the skillet to the rice. Bring to a boil, reduce the heat, cover, and simmer for 15 minutes. Add the reserved sausage and stir gently. Cover and simmer 10 minutes longer or until the rice is just tender. Gently stir in the remaining parsley, reserved peppers, chicken, and seafood. Heat briefly just to warm all the ingredients. Remove from the heat and let stand, covered, for 5 to 10 minutes to allow flavors to blend.

If Rhino Chasers® American Amber Ale is not available, see Substitution Chart.

Poultry, Rabbit, & Feathered Game

*The versatility of beer as an ingredient is very apparent in
the preparation of poultry and game. On the one hand,
the pronounced maltiness of a brown ale or a dark lager can be used to add
character to a humble chicken soup. On the other, a dry India Pale Ale or a
tart pilsner can rise to the occasion when confronted with aristocratic game
such as pheasant or venison. Braise any kind of game in a well-hopped
brew and you will find that the meat remains moist while the malt
enhances its natural flavor and the hops offset the sometimes cloying
richness that comes with aging.*

SAUTÉED CHICKEN IN BEER

4 SERVINGS

*Fresh egg noodles would be the perfect accompaniment
to this richly flavored chicken entree.*

3 to 4	pounds chicken parts
	Salt and freshly ground pepper, to taste
3	tablespoons unsalted butter
2 ½	cups Rhino Chasers® Lager beer
1	medium onion, *chopped*
1	large clove garlic, *minced*
1	bay leaf
2	whole cloves
1	tablespoon all-purpose flour
	Dash of freshly grated nutmeg
3	egg yolks, *lightly beaten*
1	cup heavy cream

Season the chicken with salt and pepper. In a large skillet, melt 2 tablespoons of the butter over medium heat. Sauté the chicken until golden brown on all sides, about 10 minutes.

Add the beer, onion, garlic, bay leaf, and cloves. Bring to a boil, reduce the heat to a simmer, and cook 35 to 45 minutes, or until the chicken is tender. Remove the chicken to a serving platter and cover to keep warm.

Over medium heat, gently boil the beer mixture to reduce by one third, about 6 minutes. Strain and discard the solids. Let the liquid stand, then spoon off and discard the excess fat that rises to the top.

In a saucepan, melt the remaining 1 tablespoon of butter over medium heat. Stir in the flour and cook for 2 minutes, stirring constantly. Gradually add the reserved liquid and the nutmeg. Simmer gently 10 minutes longer.

In a large bowl, combine the beaten egg yolks and the cream. Whisking constantly, slowly add the hot sauce. Return to the saucepan and, whisking constantly, reheat the sauce slowly over low heat. Do not boil. Pour over the chicken and serve.

If Rhino Chasers® Lager beer is not available, see Substitution Chart.

FALLEN LEAF ROTISSERIE CHICKEN

6 TO 8 SERVINGS

The aroma of this chicken as it cooks slowly on the
barbecue is likely to bring over the neighbors.

1	(4-pound) roasting chicken
2	teaspoons paprika
1	teaspoon salt
1	teaspoon freshly ground pepper
1	lemon, *halved*
½	medium onion
3	large sprigs fresh rosemary, or 1 small bunch fresh thyme
2	(12-ounce) bottles Rhino Chasers® American Amber Ale
½	cup butter
	Hickory or fruitwood chips, for smoking
1	bunch watercress, for garnish

Rinse the chicken and pat dry. Remove any excess fat. Combine the paprika, salt, and pepper.
Rub the cavity of the chicken with about half of the spice mixture. Stuff with lemon, onion,
and rosemary or thyme. Truss the legs and wings securely with twine. Thread, balance, and
secure the chicken onto a rotisserie spit. Rub the outside of the chicken with the remaining
spice mixture. Let stand at room temperature while preparing the grill or barbecue.

Add the ale, 1 cup water, and butter to a drip pan (an 8 x 8 x 2-inch baking pan
works well) and place on or among the coals. Always keep an eye on the liquid level in the
drip pan, adding more ale and water if the liquid runs low. Add the hickory chips to the
coals. Place the chicken on the grill above glowing coals or on low heat if using a gas
barbecue. Cover and cook for 1 ½ to 2 hours *(see Note)*, basting with the ale mixture in the
drip pan during the last 30 minutes. The chicken is done when the juices run clear when
pierced with a fork.

Let stand 15 minutes before carving. Remove and discard the fat from the liquid in
the drip pan. If more than 1 cup liquid remains, pour it into a small saucepan and reduce to 1
cup over medium heat. Carve the chicken into serving pieces and arrange on a bed of
watercress. Serve with the reduced sauce.

If Rhino Chasers® American Amber Ale is not available, see Substitution Chart.

CHEF
TAMARA THOMAS

PRESIDENT,
FINE ARTS
SERVICES, INC.
LOS ANGELES, CA

Note:
Cooking times will
vary according to the
temperature of the
coals, the heat
setting of the gas
barbecue, the
chicken's size, and
weather conditions.
Use a meat
thermometer to
determine doneness,
if possible.
The breast meat is
done at 170°F., dark
meat at 180°F.

CHICKEN IN STOUT

6 SERVINGS

This richly flavored dish of mushrooms, pearl onions, and chicken is a perfect company dinner when served over a bed of egg noodles.

20	pearl onions
3	tablespoons olive oil
2	tablespoons butter
6	boneless, skinless chicken breast halves
¼	cup gin
2	tablespoons all-purpose flour
1 ½	cups San Quentin® Stout
½	pound mushrooms, *sliced*
	Salt and freshly ground pepper, *to taste*
¼	cup heavy cream
1	tablespoon chopped fresh Italian parsley

To peel the onions, in a small saucepan, bring 2 cups of water to a boil. Drop in the onions and boil 3 minutes. Drain and transfer to a bowl of cold water. Cut off the root and stem ends and gently squeeze the onion out of its skin.

In a large skillet, heat the olive oil and butter over medium heat. Sauté the onions until lightly browned; remove and set aside. Add the chicken and lightly brown on both sides. Reduce the heat to low and pour in the gin. Carefully set aflame with a lit match. With tongs remove and set aside the chicken.

Sprinkle the flour into the hot skillet and cook 1 to 2 minutes, stirring constantly. Gradually pour in the stout, stirring until the sauce is smooth. Add the mushrooms, sautéed onions, salt, and pepper and bring to a boil. Return the chicken breasts to the pan. Reduce the heat to low, cover, and simmer 10 to 12 minutes, or until the chicken is tender. Remove the chicken breasts to a serving platter and keep warm. Spoon off any excess fat from the sauce and stir in the cream. Over medium heat, boil the sauce to reduce it by half, about 10 minutes. Spoon the sauce over the chicken breasts, sprinkle with the chopped parsley, and serve.

If San Quentin® stout is not available, see Substitution Chart.

CHICKEN AND VEGETABLE PHYLLO SQUARES

4 SERVINGS

This elegant package of flaky pastry with baked chicken and vegetables is a terrific dinner party choice. All it takes is a green salad and dessert to complete the meal.

CHEF
CLAUDE-ALAIN
SOLLIARD

RAOUL'S
NEW YORK, NY

1	(12-ounce) bottle New Amsterdam® beer
½	teaspoon curry powder
1	teaspoon salt
1/4	teaspoon freshly ground pepper
4	boneless, skinless chicken breast halves
8	sprigs fresh tarragon
2	teaspoons butter
¼	cup chopped shallots
¼	cup diced carrots
¼	cup diced celery
¼	cup diced fresh shiitake mushroom caps
2	(14 x 18-inch) sheets phyllo dough *(see Note)*
2	tablespoons melted butter
1	teaspoon cornstarch
1	teaspoon tomato paste
	Salt and freshly ground pepper, to taste

Combine the first six ingredients in a glass dish. Marinate overnight in the refrigerator.

Preheat the oven to 400°F. Melt the butter in a medium skillet over medium heat. Sauté the shallots, carrots, celery, and mushrooms, until soft, about 7 minutes. Set aside. Season with salt and pepper.

Lightly oil a 9 x 12-inch flameproof casserole. Transfer the chicken to the casserole, reserving the marinade. Divide the vegetables and place them on top of the chicken breasts.

Spread one sheet of phyllo on the counter and brush it with some of the melted butter. Cover it with the second sheet of phyllo. With a sharp knife, cut the dough into four rectangles. Place the dough over the vegetables and set the pan in the oven. Bake 15 minutes, until the pastry is golden brown. Transfer the chicken and pastry to a serving platter.

Note: Phyllo dough is readily available frozen in 1-pound boxes. Follow the package directions for thawing. The remaining dough should be well covered in plastic wrap and can then be stored in the refrigerator for up to 1 week.

Mix the cornstarch and 2 tablespoons water together in a small bowl. Place the baking pan with its juices over low heat and pour in 1 cup of the reserved marinade, the cornstarch mixture, and the tomato paste. Stir well, scraping the bottom of the pan, and simmer until slightly thickened, about 2 to 3 minutes. Pour the sauce over the chicken and garnish with the remaining tarragon sprigs. Serve immediately.

If New Amsterdam® beer is not available, see Substitution Chart.

GRILLED CHICKEN

*Beer and lime juice give chicken just the right dash of acidity
in this carefree summer dish.*

3   (12-ounce) bottles Anchor Steam® beer
4   teaspoons mint jelly
8   chicken legs with thighs
     Salt and freshly ground pepper, to taste
6   limes, *cut in half*
     Lime wedges, for garnish

Preheat a grill or barbecue.

Combine one bottle of beer and the mint jelly in small saucepan. Cook over low heat just to dissolve the jelly. Place the chicken in a glass or ceramic pan, pour in the beer mixture, cover, and marinate in the refrigerator for 1 hour or longer.

Remove chicken from the marinade and season it with salt and pepper. Transfer the marinade to a spray bottle and fill with remaining beer as needed. Grill the chicken skin side-up, spraying it with beer every few minutes and turning it frequently, until the juices run clear, about 25 minutes. Season with lime juice during the last 15 minutes and garnish with lime wedges.

If Anchor Steam® beer is not available, see Substitution Chart.

CHEF
BARRY WINE

RESTAURANT CITY/
WORLD WIDE WEB
NEW YORK, NY

POULTRY, RABBIT,
& FEATHERGAME
97

HINDY'S BEER CHICKEN

4 SERVINGS

*Stir the leftover juices into wild rice and serve with chicken
for a lovely weeknight dinner.*

2 ¼	cups Brooklyn® Lager or Brooklyn® Brown Ale
3	tablespoons dried tarragon leaves, *crushed*
2	tablespoons dried parsley, *crushed*
1	tablespoon poultry seasoning
	Salt and freshly ground pepper, to taste
1	(2 ½- to 3 ½-pound) broiler-fryer chicken, *quartered or cut into serving-size pieces*

In a medium bowl, whisk together all the ingredients except the chicken. Place the chicken pieces in a glass baking dish just large enough to hold them. Pour the beer mixture over the chicken. Cover and marinate in the refrigerator for 24 hours, turning the chicken pieces occasionally to marinate evenly.

To cook, preheat the oven to 350°F. Bake the chicken, uncovered, skin side up, in the baking dish with its marinade, basting every 20 minutes, for about 1 hour, or until the chicken is tender and the juices run clear when pierced with a fork.

If Brooklyn® Lager or Brooklyn® Brown Ale is not available, see Substitution Chart.

CHICKEN BREASTS WITH
ALE AND CUMIN

4 SERVINGS

*Here's a typical French chicken sauté that is big in flavor,
yet easy and quick to prepare.*

4	boneless chicken breast halves with skin
½	teaspoon ground cumin
2	tablespoons vegetable oil
¼	teaspoon minced garlic
¼	teaspoon minced shallot
¼	cup Rhino Chasers® American Amber Ale
¼	cup heavy cream
2	tablespoons Worcestershire sauce
	Salt and freshly ground pepper, to taste
	Finely chopped fresh Italian parsley, for garnish

Sprinkle both sides of the chicken with the cumin. Heat the oil in a large skillet over medium heat. Sauté the chicken until golden brown and cooked thoroughly, 5 to 7 minutes per side. Remove the chicken to a serving platter and keep warm. Add the garlic and shallots to the pan drippings and sauté briefly. Add the ale and cook to reduce slightly, about 5 minutes. Add the cream and Worcestershire sauce and cook until syrupy, about 5 minutes. Season with salt and pepper to taste. Spoon the sauce over the chicken, sprinkle with the parsley, and serve.

If Rhino Chasers® American Amber Ale is not available, see Substitution Chart.

JALAPEÑO CHICKEN WITH ALE, ALMONDS, AND RAISINS

6 SERVINGS

Although the Mexican influence is strong in this dish, the ale gives it a distinctive character. Soaking the raisins in the morning will give you a head start before beginning to cook.

⅓	cup Rhino Chasers® American Amber Ale
3	tablespoons golden raisins
2	tablespoons slivered almonds
½	pound top-quality chorizo sausage links, *sliced ½-inch thick*
2 to 3	tablespoons vegetable oil
4 to 4 ½	pounds chicken pieces
1	large onion, *thinly sliced*
1	small jalapeño chile, *seeded and finely chopped*
1	pound tomatoes, *peeled, seeded, and pureed (see Note, page 73)*
½	cup chicken stock or broth
3	medium cloves garlic, *minced*
¼	cup freshly squeezed lime juice
¾	pound zucchini, unpeeled, *cut into 2-inch julienne strips*
½	pound carrots, *cut into 2-inch julienne strips*
1	tablespoon jalapeño jelly
	Salt and freshly ground pepper, to taste

In a small saucepan, heat the ale to simmering and add the raisins. Cover and let sit at room temperature for 3 to 4 hours.

Preheat the oven to 350°F. Lightly toast the almonds in a small baking pan, shaking the pan occasionally for 7 to 10 minutes. Set aside.

In a large skillet over medium heat, sauté the chorizo until crisp and well cooked. Remove and drain on paper towels. Pour off and discard the pan drippings. In the same skillet, heat the oil over medium to high heat. In two batches, brown the chicken pieces well on all sides, about 8 to 10 minutes. Remove and set aside. Add the onion and jalapeño and sauté until soft, about 5 minutes. Remove and set aside.

Drain off and discard any excess fat from the pan. Pour the ale from the raisins (reserve the raisins) into the skillet and heat, stirring to loosen any browned bits from the bottom of the skillet. Over medium heat, reduce the liquid to a syrup, about 3 minutes. Add the pureed tomatoes, chicken stock, and garlic; cook over medium-high heat for 5 minutes, stirring occasionally. Return the chicken and chorizo to the skillet and add the lime juice. Cover and simmer 25 minutes. Add the zucchini, carrots, the reserved onion mixture, jalapeño jelly, salt, and pepper. Stir well to blend the ingredients. Cover and simmer about 20 minutes longer, or until chicken and vegetables are tender.

Stir in the raisins and half the almonds. Arrange the chicken, chorizo, and vegetables on a large serving platter. Spoon the sauce over all and sprinkle with the remaining almonds.

If Rhino Chasers® American Amber Ale is not available, see Substitution Chart.

SMOKY MOLE WITH CORNMEAL CHICKEN

8 SERVINGS

Searing the chicken breasts before baking ensures moist chicken inside and a crispy coating outside.

SMOKY MOLE

½	cup pine nuts
1 ½	corn tortillas, *coarsely chopped*
3	Roma (Italian plum) tomatoes, *halved*
3	medium cloves garlic
2	dried chipotle chiles
2	dried ancho chiles
2	dried apricot halves
4	teaspoons minced fresh ginger
2 ½	cups chicken stock or broth
½	cup Rhino Chasers® American Amber Ale
¼	cup honey
3	tablespoons freshly squeezed lime juice
¼	teaspoon ground cumin
¼	teaspoon ground coriander
½	cup chocolate chips
½	cup chopped cilantro

Preheat the oven to 350°F. Place the pine nuts, tortillas, tomatoes, garlic, chiles, apricots, and ginger on a baking sheet and bake for 5 to 10 minutes, or until the chiles puff up a bit and are toasty. In a saucepot, combine the toasted ingredients with the chicken stock, ale, honey, lime juice, cumin, and coriander. Bring to a boil, reduce the heat to a simmer, and cook, covered, for 20 minutes. Stir in the chocolate chips and the cilantro. Remove from the heat and cool slightly. In a blender, puree the mixture until smooth. Return the mole to the saucepot and reheat before serving.

1	cup stone-ground cornmeal
½	teaspoon salt
½	teaspoon cayenne pepper
8	boneless, skinless chicken breast halves
½	cup peanut oil
½	cup cilantro sprigs, for garnish

In a shallow dish, combine the cornmeal, salt, and cayenne pepper. Coat the chicken breasts well on both sides with the cornmeal mixture and place on a parchment-lined baking sheet. Lightly cover with plastic wrap and refrigerate to set the coating, at least 30 minutes.

Preheat oven to 350°F. In a large, heavy skillet, heat half the oil over medium-high heat. Sear half the chicken breasts in the oil on both sides. Place on the baking sheet (paper removed) and repeat with the remaining chicken breasts and oil. Bake the chicken in the preheated oven for 8 to 12 minutes, or until it is tender. To serve, place the chicken on serving plates and top with the warm mole sauce. Garnish with the cilantro.

If Rhino Chasers® American Amber Ale is not available, see Substitution Chart.

LORETTA HWONG-
GRIFFITHS

COOKBOOK EDITOR

STUDIO CITY, CA

SMOKIN' RHINO CHICKEN CHILI

6 SERVINGS

This is a wonderful marriage of two recipe ideas, inspired by Diane Worthington's Chicken Chili (The Taste of Summer) and Tara Thomas' Smokey Mole sauce (page 106), however, your own favorite mole sauce may be substituted.

4	tablespoons vegetable oil
2	pounds boneless, skinless chicken breast halves, *cut into 1-inch pieces*
2	medium onions, *chopped*
1	cup diced celery
3	tablespoons minced garlic
1	(12-ounce) bottle Rhino Chasers® American Amber Ale
½	cup chicken stock or broth
1	(14-ounce) can diced tomatoes, with liquid
2	tablespoons barley malt syrup
½	cup Smoky Mole *(see Headnote)*
½	teaspoon crushed, dried chipotle chili *(see Note)*
1	(15-ounce) can black beans, *rinsed and drained*
1	cup canned pinto beans, *rinsed and drained*
½	teaspoon salt, or to taste
	Pepper, to taste
	Sour cream, diced tomato, red onion, chopped cilantro leaves, sliced jalapeño peppers, grated Cheddar cheese, and lime wedges for garnish

Note:
Barley malt syrup is available in health food or gourmet food stores. It is a grain-sweetened sweetener that is stronger in flavor than honey, but milder than molasses.

Crushed red chile flakes can be substituted for the dried chipotle chile.

Heat 2 tablespoons of the oil in a large saucepan over medium-high heat. Add the chicken and sauté until just browned, about 5 minutes. Remove and set aside. Heat the remaining 2 tablespoons of oil and sauté the onions and celery over medium heat until just tender, about 3 to 5 minutes. Add the garlic and sauté 1 minute longer. Add the beer, chicken stock, and tomatoes, scraping the pan's bottom to loosen any browned bits. Add the barley malt syrup. Bring to a boil; reduce to a simmer and cook covered, for 20 minutes. Add the smoky mole and dried chile. Simmer, covered, 20 minutes longer. Add the beans and chicken and simmer, uncovered, another 30 minutes to reduce the liquid slightly. Season with salt and pepper to taste and cook for another 10 minutes. Ladle into serving bowls and garnish, as desired.

If Rhino Chasers® American Amber Ale is not available, see Substitution Chart.

TURKEY AND BLACK BEAN CHILI WITH ROASTED ANCHO CHILES

6 TO 8 SERVINGS

This chili is best made ahead and reheated. It also freezes well, so double the recipe if you have a pot big enough. Serve topped with shredded Panela, a Mexican-imported cheese or Mozzarella and diced red onion.

3	dried ancho chiles, *rinsed*
1	head garlic, *separated into cloves and peeled*
2 ½	pounds ground turkey
2	cups finely chopped celery
1	large onion, *finely chopped*
2 to 3	tablespoons olive oil
2 ½	cups Dos Equis® beer, plus additional to moisten (optional)
2 ½	cups chopped fresh or canned tomatoes, *drained and juice reserved*
½	cup strong brewed coffee
2	tablespoons each ground cumin, ground coriander, and chili powder, *lightly toasted (see Note)*
	Salt and freshly ground pepper, to taste
	Chicken broth to moisten (optional)
2	cups cooked dried black beans or 1 (15-ounce) can, *drained*

Slit open the chiles and remove and discard the seeds and stems (if your skin is sensitive, wear rubber gloves). Soak the chiles in a bowl of hot water 30 to 45 minutes, or until soft. In a blender or food processor, puree the drained chiles and garlic, adding a little bit of the chile soaking water to form a smooth paste. Set aside.

In a large saucepan over medium-high heat, lightly brown the turkey, celery, and onion in the oil, stirring frequently. Add the chili-garlic puree and all the remaining ingredients except the chicken broth (if using) and the black beans. Bring to a boil, then reduce the heat, partially cover, and simmer, stirring occasionally, for about 1 hour. Check the liquid level and add beer, chicken stock, or water, if necessary, to moisten. Stir in the beans and simmer 20 minutes longer.

If Dos Equis® beer is not available, see Substitution Chart.

Note:
To toast dried spices, combine them in a small nonstick skillet and cook over medium to high heat for 2 to 3 minutes, stirring often, or place in a preheated 350° F. oven for 3 to 4 minutes, stirring once or twice.

CHEF
VINCENT E. KIKUGAWA

PARADISE
GARDENA, CA

PARADISE CAFÉ
NORTH HOLLYWOOD, CA

OVEN—BRAISED TURKEY BREAST PENNSYLVANIA

4 TO 6 SERVINGS

If you love turkey but would like a change from the plain roasted bird, look no further. The cream-enriched sauce is excellent over rice or mashed potatoes.

1	half turkey breast (2 to 3 pounds), with back and ribs
1	tablespoon olive oil
2	tablespoons butter
1	medium onion, *chopped*
½	pound tomatoes, *peeled, seeded, and chopped*
½	cup raisins
1	(12-ounce) bottle Rhino Chasers® Lager beer
¾	cup heavy cream
2	egg yolks
	Salt and freshly ground white pepper, to taste

Preheat the oven to 325°F. Rinse and pat dry the turkey. Remove any excess fat. In a large ovenproof casserole, over medium heat, lightly brown the turkey on all sides in the olive oil and 1 tablespoon of the butter. Remove and set aside. Sauté the onion in the pan drippings with the remaining 1 tablespoon butter until soft. Add the tomatoes and raisins and cook briefly. Stir in the beer and bring to a boil. Add the turkey, bone side down, cover, and bake in the preheated oven for 35 to 50 minutes, or until the internal temperature reaches 170°F. on a meat thermometer. Remove the turkey breast and set it aside to cool slightly, reserving the pan juices. Reduce the oven temperature to low. Remove the turkey from the bones by cutting from the backbone down along the ribs to loosen the breast meat in one piece. Keep warm in the low oven.

Meanwhile, to make the sauce, strain the pan juices and return the juices to the casserole *(see Note)*. In a small bowl, whisk together the cream and egg yolks. Set the pan over low heat and slowly add the cream mixture, stirring constantly until the sauce thickens slightly. Season with salt and pepper to taste. Slice the turkey breast crosswise and serve with the sauce.

If Rhino Chasers® Lager beer is not available, see Substitution Chart.

Note:
For a chunkier sauce, add the strained raisin-tomato mixture back into the thickened sauce. Or garnish sauce with ⅓ cup of toasted, finely chopped almonds.

POULTRY, RABBIT, & FEATHERGAME
106

KARINA'S GOURMET MEAT LOAF

6 SERVINGS

KARINA KANSKY

PERFORMER,
COMPOSER,
FASHION,
AND
JEWELRY
DESIGNER
SAN FRANCISCO, CA

Garlic mashed potatoes and buttered carrots would be heaven alongside this delicious meat loaf.

1	tablespoon olive oil
1	medium onion, *chopped*
1	large carrot, *grated*
3	tablespoons minced fresh Italian parsley
½	cup Rhino Chasers® American Amber Ale
1	beef bouillon cube
3	tablespoons ketchup
PINCH	cayenne pepper
PINCH	poultry seasoning
1	cup herbed stuffing mix
1	pound ground turkey
½	pound ground beef
2	eggs, *beaten*
¼	cup currant jelly or jam
⅔	cup chili sauce
2	tablespoons black currants
½	teaspoon dry mustard

Preheat the oven to 350°F. Heat the olive oil in large skillet over medium to high heat. Sauté the onion, carrot, and parsley until soft, about 7 minutes. Set aside

In a small saucepan, combine the beer and bouillon cube. Bring to a boil and dissolve the bouillon cube. Remove from heat and stir in the ketchup, cayenne, poultry seasoning, and stuffing mix, until evenly moistened.

In a large mixing bowl, combine the turkey and beef. Add the eggs, onion mixture, and stuffing mixture. Mix well. Pat into a generously greased 9 x 5 x 3-inch loaf pan.

Combine the remaining ingredients in small saucepan and boil until smooth. Pour over the meat loaf and bake 1 hour. Let sit 5 minutes before slicing and serving.

If Rhino Chasers® American Amber Ale is not available, see Substitution Chart.

LAMBIC—MARINATED RABBIT STEW À LA BROOKS

4 TO 6 SERVINGS

This is the rabbit dish to serve to people who claim not to like rabbit. The fruit flavors blend to make an unbelievably delicious entree.

1	(2 ½-pound) rabbit, *cut into serving-size pieces*
2	teaspoons celery salt
	Freshly ground pepper and ground coriander, to taste
	Dash of nutmeg and crushed dried thyme leaves
2	cups Cantillon® or Oud Beersel® Gueuze or Kriek® beer
2	tablespoons cider vinegar
2	bay leaves
¼	pound bacon, *diced*
4	tablespoons butter
10	medium shallots, *minced*
3	medium cloves garlic, *minced*
2	tablespoons Dijon mustard
4	medium carrots, *sliced ½ inch thick*
½	pound pitted prunes
¼	cup milk
1 ½	tablespoons cornstarch
3	tablespoons orange marmalade

Rub the rabbit all over with the celery salt, pepper, coriander, nutmeg, and thyme. Place in a large bowl. Add the beer, vinegar, and bay leaves. Cover and marinate in the refrigerator 12 to 24 hours, turning occasionally to marinate evenly.

In a large saucepot, fry the bacon in 1 tablespoon of the butter over medium heat until crisp. Add the shallots and sauté until soft, about 3 minutes. Remove the bacon and shallots with a slotted spoon and set aside. Remove the rabbit from the marinade and pat dry with paper towels, reserving the marinade.

In batches, add the rabbit pieces to the fat remaining in the pan and brown well on all sides, about 6 to 8 minutes, using the remaining 3 tablespoons of butter as needed. Remove the rabbit and set aside. Add ¼ cup of the reserved marinade to the pan and cook, stirring to loosen any browned bits from the bottom. Add the garlic and cook to reduce the liquid by half, about 3 minutes.

Return the rabbit and the bacon and shallot mixture to the pan. Add the remaining reserved marinade (with the bay leaves) and the mustard. Bring to a boil, stirring occasionally. Reduce to a simmer and cook, covered, for 1 hour. Add the carrots and prunes; cover and cook 1 hour longer, or until the rabbit and carrots are tender. Remove the rabbit and set aside.

Combine the milk and cornstarch and gradually stir it into the pan. Cook over medium-high heat, stirring until the sauce thickens, about 3 minutes. Add the marmalade, stirring to blend well. Return the rabbit to the pan to reheat. Remove and discard the bay leaves before serving.

If Cantillon® or Oud Beersel® Gueuze or Kriek® beer is not available, see Substitution Chart.

CHEF
RICHARD MOSKOVITZ

DEERFIELD BEACH/
BOCA RATON
HILTON HOTEL
DEERFIELD BEACH, FL

SOY AND MOLASSES DUCK WITH GREEN CABBAGE

4 SERVINGS

Thinly sliced duck is served over a highly infused cabbage mixture.

2	whole duck breasts (about 1 pound each), *halved*
½	cup molasses
¼	cup light soy sauce
1	pound fatback bacon, *cut into thin strips, blanched for 10 minutes, and drained*
2	medium onions, *sliced*
10	medium shallots, *halved*
2	tablespoons thinly sliced garlic
1	small head cabbage, *thinly sliced*
1	(12-ounce) bottle Samuel Smith Nut Brown Ale®
2	cups drained diced tomatoes, *juice reserved separately*
1	small bunch fresh marjoram leaves, *chopped*, plus whole fresh marjoram leaves for garnish (optional)
	Salt and freshly ground pepper, to taste

Place the duck breasts, skin side down, in a large skillet. Over low heat, render the fat for 45 to 60 minutes. Reserve ¼ cup of the duck fat, discarding the rest.

In a large bowl combine the molasses and soy sauce. Add the duck breasts and marinate for 30 minutes, turning them occasionally to coat all sides.

To prepare the cabbage, in a large saucepot, heat the reserved duck fat over medium heat. Add fatback and cook, stirring occasionally until the pieces begin to crisp, about 10 minutes. Add the onions, shallots, and garlic and sauté 5 minutes. Add the cabbage and sauté 5 minutes longer. Pour in the ale, the reserved tomato juices, and 2 to 4 tablespoons of the marinade from the duck. Cook, uncovered, over medium heat, stirring occasionally until the cabbage is just tender, about 20 minutes. Stir in the tomatoes, chopped marjoram, salt, and pepper and cook an additional 5 minutes.

Preheat a grill or barbecue. Grill or barbecue the duck breasts over glowing coals or on medium to high heat, cut side down, 3 to 5 minutes for medium to rare, or 10 minutes for well done. Turn and quickly sear, skin side down, 1 to 2 minutes. Remove and let rest about 3 minutes before slicing.

   To serve, thinly slice each duck breast lengthwise. Spoon portions of the cabbage mixture onto each serving plate. Fan the duck slices over the cabbage. Garnish with fresh marjoram leaves, if desired.

   If Samuel Smith Nut Brown Ale® is not available, see Substitution Chart.

INTOXICATED QUAIL

4 SERVINGS

These little birds take a bath in beer before being cooked to perfection and served with a balsamic vinegar and beer sauce.

4	semi-boned quail, wing tips trimmed, *rinsed and patted dry*
1	(12-ounce) bottle Rhino Chasers® Lager beer
8	fresh sage leaves
4	slices bacon, preferably applewood-smoked
	Salt and freshly ground white pepper, to taste
½	cup balsamic vinegar
2	tablespoons golden raisins
¼	cup olive oil
2	tablespoons pine nuts, *toasted*

Place the quail in a large bowl. Pour in 1 cup of the beer and marinate in the refrigerator, turning twice, for 30 minutes. Remove the quail and pat dry with paper towels. Discard the marinade.

Place two sage leaves on the breast of each quail. Wrap each breast tightly with 1 slice of bacon (a toothpick may be useful to keep it tightly wrapped). Season with salt and pepper to taste.

To cook, preheat a grill or barbecue *(see Note)*. Preheat the oven to 400°F. Grill or barbecue the quail, breast side down over glowing coals or medium heat until nicely browned, 5 to 8 minutes. Transfer, breast side up, to a large, flameproof roasting pan and bake 8 to 10 minutes, or until the breast meat is firm, yet springy when pressed with the back of a spoon.

Remove the quail and keep warm. Place the baking pan on a top burner and add the balsamic vinegar, the remaining ½ cup of beer, and the raisins. Cook over medium heat to reduce the liquid to one third, about 7 minutes. Add the olive oil and stir briskly. Remove from the heat.

Cut the quail in half and arrange two halves on each serving plate. Drizzle each with some sauce and sprinkle with the pine nuts.

If Rhino Chasers® Lager beer is not available, see Substitution Chart.

Note:
Instead of grilling or barbecuing, the quail can be sautéed before baking. Heat a large skillet, lightly coated with vegetable oil, and sauté the quail breast side down over medium heat until golden brown, about 5 to 8 minutes. Remove from the skillet and place breast side up in the baking pan and proceed as above.

POULTRY, RABBIT,
& FEATHERGAME

112

BARBECUED QUAIL IN BEER MARINADE

4 SERVINGS

*Don't be afraid to pick up these little birds with your fingers
and nibble at their bones.*

8	quail, *cleaned, rinsed and patted dry*
1	(12-ounce) bottle Rhino Chasers® Lager beer
¼	cup ketchup
2	tablespoons brown sugar
2	tablespoons raspberry vinegar
2	tablespoons Tabasco sauce
2	tablespoons honey
2	medium cloves garlic, *minced*
	Salt and freshly ground pepper, to taste

Place the quail in a large bowl and pour in the beer. Cover and marinate in the refrigerator
for 6 hours or overnight.

Preheat a grill or barbecue. To make the basting sauce, combine all the remaining
ingredients and ¼ cup of the beer from the marinade in a small bowl. Place the quail, breast
side down, on the grill above glowing coals or on high heat if using a gas barbecue. Brush
the tops with the sauce, and cook 4 minutes. Turn and brush the second side with sauce;
cook another 4 minutes. Reduce the heat to low or move quail to a cooler spot on the grill or
barbecue. Continue cooking 15 to 30 minutes, turning and basting often with the sauce
until the juices run clear.

If Rhino Chasers® Lager beer is not available, see Substitution Chart.

Meat

Meat and beer are such a sterling combination
that it's astonishing it isn't celebrated with an annual holiday, or
at least a postage stamp. Certain classic meat stews, such as carbonades de
boeuf à la flamande, *depend on beer for their essential character.*
But beer can also be used to add gusto to chili, zest to baked ham, and
verve to calf's liver with caramelized onions. Try a steak au poivre *made
with barley wine in the sauce; enjoy the delicate flavor of sweetbreads
braised in lager; or simply use a pale ale to deglaze the pan in which you
have cooked lamb chops or pork cutlets.*

PORK AND NEW MEXICO SAUSAGE IN GREEN CHILI BEER SAUCE

6 TO 8 SERVINGS AS A MAIN COURSE,
OR ENOUGH FOR 8 BURRITOS, 12 SOFT TACOS, OR 18 ENCHILADAS

*Use this hearty stew as a filling for soft tacos, burritos, or enchiladas,
or serve it with rice. If making enchiladas, reserve some of the sauce
and spoon it over the enchiladas before baking.*

2	tablespoons vegetable oil
1	pound lean pork, *cut into 1-inch cubes*
	Salt and freshly ground pepper, to taste
2	pounds New Mexico sausage or spicy hot Italian sausage, *cut into ½-inch-thick rounds*
2	large onions, *coarsely chopped*
¼	cup chopped garlic
1	teaspoon ground cumin
2	cups Mexican beer such as Bohemia® or Carta Blanca®
¼	cup fresh lime juice, plus additional to taste (optional)
2	small bunches cilantro with roots
8 to 10	Anaheim green chiles, *roasted, peeled, seeded, and chopped,* or 2 (7-ounce) cans chopped green chiles

In a large skillet or Dutch oven, heat 1 tablespoon of the oil over medium-high heat. Season the pork all over with salt and pepper. Lightly brown it on all sides for about 6 minutes. Add ½ pound of the sausage and cook 1 to 2 minutes longer, stirring frequently. Remove the meats and set aside. Add the onions, garlic, and the remaining tablespoon of oil. Reduce the heat to medium and cook, stirring occasionally, about 6 minutes, until the onions are soft and translucent. Stir in the cumin, a dash of salt and pepper, and cook 1 minute longer. Add the beer, lime juice, and the cooked pork and sausage mixture. Bring to a boil, then reduce the heat to a simmer.

Finely chop the cilantro roots and stems (reserving the leaves) and add them to the simmering pork mixture. Stir in the chiles. Simmer, uncovered, for 45 to 60 minutes, until the pork is tender. Add the remaining sausage and cook 10 minutes longer. Coarsely chop the cilantro leaves and add all but ¼ cup to the meat mixture. Cook 5 minutes longer. Season with salt, pepper, and additional lime juice, to taste. Garnish with the remaining ¼ cup chopped cilantro.

❋

If Bohemia® or Carta Blanca® beer is not available, see Substitution Chart.

ITALIAN BEER SAUSAGE WITH PEPPERS AND ONIONS

4 SERVINGS

Sausage and beer are a natural duet, and in this recipe, confetti strips of red and green add a dramatic note.

4	tablespoons cooking oil
2	cups green peppers, *cut into 3-inch julienned strips*
2	cups red peppers, *cut into 3-inch julienned strips*
3	cups onion, *julienned*
8	Italian sausage (4-ounce)
3	cups Rhino Chasers® Dark Roasted Läger
6	tablespoons sweet butter
2	teaspoons lemon juice
	Salt and freshly ground pepper, to taste

To a 10-inch skillet, add 2 tablespoons oil over medium-high heat and sauté the green and red peppers, stirring occasionally for approximately 12 minutes or until browned. Remove the peppers, place in a separate bowl and set aside.

To the same skillet, add 2 tablespoon of oil and sauté the onion over medium heat for 2 minutes. Add the sausages and cook together until the sausages are medium-rare, about 10 minutes. Deglaze the skillet with the beer and simmer about 20 minutes, reducing the liquid to about 1 cup. Remove the sausages and keep warm. Using a slotted spoon, remove the onions and mix them with the sautéed peppers. Arrange the onion mixture on a warmed serving platter and top with the sausages.

Meanwhile, bring the liquid in the skillet back to a simmer. Add the butter and the lemon juice and whisk until slightly thickened, about 3 minutes (do not overcook or the butter will separate). Season with salt and pepper and pour over the sausages.

If Rhino Chasers® Dark Roasted Läger is not available, see Substitution Chart.

CHOUCROUTE

*Serve this hearty entree with small boiled potatoes,
good rye bread, and a variety of spicy mustards.*

½	pound bacon, *diced*
2	Roma (Italian plum) tomatoes, *chopped*
1	large onion, *thinly sliced*
1	tablespoon caraway seeds
	Dash of salt
2	pounds imported German sauerkraut, *drained*
4	frankfurters
2	knockwursts (4 ounces each)
2	bockwursts (weisswurst) (4 ounces each)
2	bauerwursts (4 ounces each)
1	(12-ounce) bottle Becks® beer

In a large saucepot, fry the bacon over medium heat 4 to 5 minutes, stirring occasionally.
Add the tomatoes, onion, caraway seeds, and salt and cook 5 minutes longer. Add the
drained sauerkraut and stir to mix well. Remove half the sauerkraut and set aside. Pierce
the sausages in several places with a fork to keep them from bursting during cooking.
Arrange the sausages over the sauerkraut mixture in the saucepot. Place the remaining
sauerkraut over the sausages. Pour in the beer and bring to a boil. Reduce the heat to
a simmer and cook, covered, for 1 hour.

If Becks® beer is not available, see Substitution Chart.

IMPERIAL STOUT WILD MUSHROOM SAUTÉ WITH BRAISED LAMB SAUSAGES

4 SERVINGS

The richness of the Imperial Stout makes this one of the tastiest pasta dishes ever.

2	pounds wild mushrooms (portobello, shiitake, and/or hedgehog), *cleaned and cut into large chunks*
¼	cup plus 3 tablespoons olive oil
2	bunches scallions, *chopped*
½	cup chopped fresh herbs such as Italian parsley, rosemary, and sage
4	large cloves garlic, *minced*
1 ¼	cups Samuel Smith® Imperial Stout
½	cup beef, chicken, lamb, or mushroom stock
1	pound lamb sausage, *sliced ¼ inch thick*
	Hot cooked fettuccine or spaghetti
	Fresh Italian parsley sprigs, for garnish

In a large skillet over medium heat, sauté the mushrooms in ¼ cup of the olive oil until the mushrooms start to give up their moisture. Add the scallions, herbs, and garlic. Sauté until the liquid has evaporated. Stir in 1 cup of the stout and the stock. Simmer a few minutes to blend the flavors.

Meanwhile, in a second large skillet over medium heat, sauté the sausage in the remaining olive oil until lightly browned and cooked through, about 8 minutes. Add the remaining ¼ cup stout and simmer a few minutes, stirring to loosen any browned bits from the bottom of the skillet. Add the sausage mixture to the mushrooms stirring well to combine. Serve over the cooked pasta, garnished with the Italian parsley sprigs.

If Samuel Smith® Imperial Stout is not available, see Substitution Chart.

DARK BEER CHORIZO SAUSAGE

6 SERVINGS

You may need a sausage grinder, or have your butcher grind the meat to make these terrific Mexican sausages.

CHEF
TIM ANDERSON

CAFE MARIMBA
BURLINGAME, CA

2	pounds boneless pork butt
½	pound fatback
½	cup Bohemia® beer
½	cup soaked, drained, and puréed ancho chiles
12	medium cloves garlic, *minced*
3	tablespoons paprika
5	teaspoons salt
1 ½	teaspoons ground coriander
1 ½	teaspoons ground Mexican oregano
1 ½	teaspoons freshly ground black pepper
1 ½	teaspoons ground red New Mexico chili
1	teaspoon ground cumin
¼	teaspoon ground cloves
¼	teaspoon ground cayenne pepper
	Pork sausage casings, *soaked and rinsed well*

Cut the pork and fatback into 2-inch cubes and, using the coarse blade of a meat grinder, grind them together. In a large bowl, combine the pork mixture with all the remaining ingredients except the pork casings and mix well. Fit a sausage stuffing attachment on the grinder and run the mixture through again, into the sausage casings. If sausage stuffing attachment is not available, use a funnel, or cake decorator without the tube attachment. Tie the casings at 4-inch intervals with kitchen twine. Cover and let sit at room temperature about 2 hours, then refrigerate. The sausages can be made 1 week ahead of time and stored in the refrigerator.

To cook, preheat the oven to 400°F. Place the sausage links in a baking pan. Prick the casings in a couple of places with a knife. Bake for about 20 minutes, turning them occasionally. Drain on paper towels, chill, and slice or cut into chunks and sauté or grill, as desired. To test for doneness, make a slit and check that no pink is remaining.

If Bohemia® beer is not available, see Substitution Chart.

PORK AND BEANS WITH STOUT

8 TO 10 SERVINGS

This is no ordinary side dish of beans with pork. It is a hearty entree like carnitas, greatly enhanced by the maltiness of the stout.

1	(4- to 5-pound) boneless pork shoulder, or 2 (2- to 2 ½-pound) pork butts
1	tablespoon vegetable oil
3	medium onions, *chopped*
¼	cup tomato paste
2	(12-ounce) bottles Rhino Chasers® American Amber Ale
2	cups Samuel Adams® Cream Stout
2	cups dried red kidney beans, *sorted and rinsed well*
1	tablespoon minced garlic
4	bay leaves
1	teaspoon ground coriander
½	teaspoon cayenne pepper
1	teaspoon salt, or to taste

Preheat the oven to 300°F. Rinse and pat dry the pork. Trim off any excess fat. In a large ovenproof casserole or Dutch oven, heat the oil over medium heat. Add the pork and brown it well on all sides. Remove the pork and set aside. Spoon off and discard any excess fat from the pan. Add the onions and tomato paste, stirring well to scrape up any browned bits. Place the pork on top of the onion mixture along with any accompanying meat juices. Cover and bake for 1 hour.

Remove the casserole from the oven leaving the oven on. Add the ale, stout, beans, garlic, bay leaves, coriander, and cayenne pepper. Bring to a boil on top of the stove, stirring occasionally. Then cover and return the casserole to the oven for 2 ½ hours, or until the beans are tender, stirring the mixture two or three times. Remove the meat and set it aside to cool slightly before slicing or cutting into chunks.

Remove and discard the bay leaves. Spoon off any excess fat from the top of the beans. Add the salt. If the liquid seems too thin, reduce it by boiling, uncovered, to the desired consistency. Serve the slices or chunks of pork with the beans.

If Rhino Chasers® American Amber Ale and Samuel Adams® Cream Stout is not available, see Substitution Chart.

HONEY—ROASTED LAMB

8 TO 10 SERVINGS

This easy roast lamb is succulent and sweet with a touch of curry,
coconut, and currants. Serve it with rice and a selection
of roasted vegetables.

1	(3 ½ - to 4-pound) boneless leg of lamb
	Salt and freshly ground pepper, to taste
1 ½	teaspoons dried mint leaves, *crushed*
1	teaspoon garlic powder
1	teaspoon curry powder
1	cup honey
1	(12-ounce) bottle Rhino Chasers® American Amber Ale
½	cup flaked or shredded coconut
½	cup currants

Season the lamb all over with salt and pepper. Sprinkle the lamb, cut side up, with 1 teaspoon of the mint and ½ teaspoon each of the garlic and curry powders. Place it in a roasting pan, cut side up, and drizzle ½ cup of the honey and ¼ cup of the ale over the lamb. Roll up the lamb and tie it securely with kitchen twine in three places. Turn it seam side down in the pan. Pour the remaining ale over the lamb. Drizzle with the remaining honey, and sprinkle with the remaining mint, and garlic and curry powders. Coat the lamb's surface with the coconut and currants. Cover and marinate in the refrigerator 1 hour or longer.

Preheat the oven to 400°F. Roast the lamb, uncovered, in the marinade for 1 ¼ to 1 ½ hours (140°F. for rare, 160°F. for medium on a meat thermometer). If the roast starts to brown too fast, tent it with aluminum foil. Baste occasionally with the pan juices during the last 20 minutes of cooking. Let the lamb rest 15 to 20 minutes before untying and carving it.

If Rhino Chasers® American Amber Ale is not available, see Substitution Chart.

DEBBIE ALLEN

ACTRESS,
DANCER,
CHOREOGRAPHER,
AND
DIRECTOR
LOS ANGELES, CA

CHEF
SHIGEFUMI TACHIBE

CHAYA BRASSERIE
LOS ANGELES, CA
CHAYA VENICE
VENICE, CA

GRILLED MONGOLIAN LAMB WITH BEER RISOTTO

4 SERVINGS

Each element of this entree has its own distinctive flavor and texture, yet they combine to create a harmonious whole.

⅔	cup Rhino Chasers® American Amber Ale
⅓	cup sweet mirin *(see Note)*
¼	cup soy sauce
1	small onion, *thinly sliced*
½	orange, *peeled and thinly sliced*
2	teaspoons minced garlic
2	teaspoons minced fresh ginger
½	jalapeño pepper, *seeded and sliced*
8	loin lamb chops
	Risotto (see below)

In a large bowl, combine the first eight ingredients. Add the lamb chops, tossing to coat them evenly. Cover and marinate in the refrigerator for 3 hours.

Preheat a grill or barbecue. Remove the lamb chops from the marinade. Pour the marinade into a saucepan and reduce it over medium heat, stirring occasionally, to one third; set aside.

Grill or barbecue the lamb chops 3 to 5 minutes per side, or to desired doneness. Serve the lamb chops over the risotto. Spoon on the reduced sauce.

RISOTTO – Makes 2 ½ cups or 4 servings

1	medium onion, *finely chopped*
3	tablespoons olive oil
2	cups short grain or Arborio rice
2 ¼	cups chicken stock or broth
¾	cup Watney's® Cream Stout
½	cup freshly grated Parmesan cheese
	Salt and freshly ground pepper, to taste

In a large heavy saucepan over medium heat, sauté the onion in the olive oil until just tender, 4 to 5 minutes. Add the rice, chicken stock, and three fourths of the stout. Bring to a boil, reduce the heat to a simmer, and cook, covered, for 20 minutes or until the rice is tender. Stir in the remaining stout, the Parmesan cheese, salt, and pepper. Serve immediately.

If Rhino Chasers® American Amber Ale and Watney's® Cream Stout is not available,
see Substitution Chart.

CHEF
WILLIAM PRUNTY

JEAN-CLAUDE
NEW YORK, NY

CAFÉ LURE
NEW YORK, NY

Note:
To prepare the leeks,
trim the roots and
dark upper leaves to
about 1 ½ inches
above the white
part and discard.
Cut the leeks in half
lengthwise and soak
or rinse well in cold
water to remove any
sand between the
leaves.

CILANTRO AND GARLIC—BRAISED LAMB SHANKS

4 SERVINGS

The lamb's wonderful juices incorporate with the other vegetables to make a simple and satisfying dish.

2	bunches cilantro
4	(1-inch-thick) lamb shanks
	Salt and freshly ground pepper, to taste
¼	pound smoked slab bacon, *cut into ½-inch cubes*
2	heads garlic, *halved crosswise*
1	cup roughly chopped celery
½	cup roughly chopped carrots
1	onion, *thinly sliced*
2	leeks, white part only, *washed and thinly sliced (see Note)*
2	teaspoons cumin seeds
¼	cup sherry vinegar
2	cups Rhino Chasers® American Amber Ale
1	cup veal or beef stock
2	medium tomatoes, *seeded and diced*
7	sprigs fresh thyme

Preheat the oven to 325°F. Wash and dry the cilantro, separating the leaves and stems. Roughly chop both, reserving ¼ cup of the chopped leaves for the sauce. Season the lamb all over with salt and pepper.

In a large roasting pan, cook the bacon over low heat until crisp. Remove it with slotted spoon and set aside to drain on paper towels. Turn the heat to high and brown the lamb on all sides. Remove and drain on paper towels.

Add the garlic, celery, carrots, onion, and leeks to the pan. Reduce the heat to low and cook until lightly browned, about 5 minutes. Stir in the cilantro leaves and stems and the cumin and cook until the aroma is released, about 2 minutes. Pour in the sherry vinegar, scraping the bottom of the pan to release any browned bits. Add the remaining ingredients (except the reserved cilantro leaves), including the reserved lamb, and bring to a simmer.

Cover and bake in the preheated oven for 45 minutes to 1 hour, until the meat is tender and falling off the bone. Reduce the oven temperature to low. Transfer the lamb to a serving platter and keep warm in the low oven.

Strain the liquid from the pan into a saucepan and bring to a boil. Cook until reduced to ¾ cup, about 10 minutes, stir in the reserved cilantro leaves, and pour over the lamb. Serve immediately.

If Rhino Chasers® American Amber Ale is not available, see Substitution Chart.

CHEF
MICHAEL NIX

PESCE FRESCO/
COPPER MOUNTAIN
RESORT,
COPPER MOUNTAIN, CO

LAMB SHANKS SALTIMBEERCO

4 SERVINGS

These tender, slow-cooked lamb shanks are enhanced
by a dash of sweet and sour.

4	lamb shanks (4 pounds)
	All-purpose flour, for dredging
¼	cup cooking oil
2	medium carrots, *julienned*
1	medium onion, *chopped*
1	celery rib, *chopped*
¼	cup chopped garlic
6	cups beef stock or broth
1	(22-ounce) bottle Jack Rabbit® Pale Ale
1	cup chopped tomatoes
¾	cup mango chutney
¼	cup champagne or white wine vinegar
¼	cup dried parsley flakes
1	teaspoon dried crushed red pepper

Coat the lamb shanks with the flour, shaking off any excess. In a large casserole or Dutch oven, heat the oil over medium-high heat and brown the shanks well on all sides. Remove the lamb and set aside. Add the carrots, onion, celery, and garlic to the pan drippings. Sauté over medium heat until the vegetables are lightly browned, about 7 minutes. Add the lamb shanks and the remaining ingredients and bring to a boil, stirring occasionally. Gently boil for 15 minutes. Reduce the heat to a simmer and cook, covered, for 2 to 2 ½ hours, until the lamb shanks are tender.

If Jack Rabbit® Pale Ale is not available, see Substitution Chart.

Note:
Thicken the sauce
with all-purpose
flour or cornstarch,
if desired, and use
as a gravy.

DUNKLES GLAZED LAMB SIRLOIN

4 SERVINGS

*Serve this elegant entree over a bed of couscous with an
array of steamed vegetables for a complete meal.*

EXECUTIVE CHEF
JEFFREY JOSEPH
ANDERSON

GORDON BIERSCH
BREWERY
RESTAURANTS
PALO ALTO,
PASADENA,
SAN FRANCISCO,
SAN JOSE, CA,
AND
HONOLULU, HI

GLAZE

¼	medium onion, *diced*
1	teaspoon minced garlic
1	tablespoon olive oil
¼	cup balsamic vinegar
2	tablespoons light brown sugar
½	cup Dunkles® Porter Bavarian-Style Dark Beer

In a small skillet over medium heat, sauté the onion and the garlic in the olive oil until
tender, about 3 minutes. Add the vinegar and the brown sugar. Cook, stirring, until reduced
to a syrup, about 3 minutes. Add the beer and bring to a boil; reduce slightly and set aside.
Reheat before serving.

LAMB

¼	cup olive oil
1	small red onion, *sliced*
6	medium cloves garlic, *minced*
4	sprigs fresh thyme
1	teaspoon freshly ground pepper
4	(¾- to 1-inch-thick) lamb sirloin steaks

Combine the first five ingredients and pour over the lamb steaks. Cover and marinate in
the refrigerator 6 hours or overnight.

Preheat a grill or gas barbecue. Remove the steaks from the marinade (discard
the marinade) and grill or barbecue over glowing coals or medium to high heat for
4 to 7 minutes on each side, or to taste.

To serve, top with the warm glaze.

If Dunkles® Porter Bavarian-Style Dark Beer is not available, see Substitution Chart.

ROASTED PORK LOIN WITH
HONEY—BEER GLAZE

8 SERVINGS

Pork at its best, roasted and infused with a fragrant blend of spices. Barley malt syrup, which blends well with beer, is a grain-sweetened sweetener that is stronger in flavor than honey but milder than molasses. It is available in health or gourmet food stores.

1	(4-pound) pork loin roast with bone *(see Note)*
2	tablespoons Roasted Seed Mixture (see below)
1	tablespoon kosher salt
1	tablespoon cracked pepper
2	cups vegetables such as carrot peels, onion, celery, and/or leek tops, *coarsely chopped*
1	(12-ounce) bottle Bohemia® beer
3	tablespoons honey
2	tablespoons barley malt syrup *(see Headnote)*

Preheat the oven to 350°F. Season the pork roast with the roasted seed mixture, salt, and pepper. Arrange the vegetable scraps in the bottom of a roasting pan and place the pork roast on top. Roast in the preheated oven for 1 hour and 20 minutes, or until a meat thermometer reads 160°F. Let rest 15 minutes before slicing.

While the pork roasts, bring the beer to a boil in a medium saucepan over medium heat. Boil until reduced by half, about 7 minutes. Add the honey and barley malt syrup and remove from the heat. Serve the sauce over the sliced pork roast.

ROASTED SEED MIXTURE – Makes ⅓ cup

3	tablespoons fennel seeds
3	tablespoons ground cumin
1	teaspoon whole cloves
1	stick Mexican cinnamon

Note:
Pork loin chops
(1 ½ inches thick)
can be substituted for
the pork roast. Grill
or barbecue over
glowing coals or
medium heat for 7 to
8 minutes on each
side, or to the desired
degree of doneness.
Serve with the sauce.

Place all the seasonings in a small, dry baking pan and roast at 350°F. for 4 to 6 minutes, or until their fragrance is released. Break the cinnamon stick into several pieces and place it, along with the other seasonings, in an electric grinder. Grind all to a powder. Store in a covered container.

If Bohemia® beer is not available, see Substitution Chart.

CHEF
BILLY HAHN

HARBORSIDE
RESTAURANT/
McCORMICK &
SCHMICK
PORTLAND, OR

ALE-BRAISED PORK CHOPS

4 SERVINGS

Whip up some garlic mashed potatoes to serve along with these tender chops and their savory sauce.

4	(1-inch-thick) center-cut loin pork chops
	All-purpose flour
2	tablespoons vegetable oil
1	medium onion, *cut into very thin wedges*
1	small shallot, *minced*
1	cup beef stock or broth
1	cup Rhino Chasers® American Amber Ale
8	dried figs, *stems removed, halved lengthwise*
1	tablespoon light brown sugar
	Salt and freshly ground pepper, to taste

Coat the pork chops with flour and shake off any excess. In a large skillet, heat the oil over medium-high heat and brown the chops well on both sides. Remove and set aside. Add the onion and the shallot and sauté over medium heat about 2 minutes. Add 1 tablespoon of flour and cook, stirring, 1 to 2 minutes longer. Gradually add the stock and ale stirring constantly.

Add the pork chops, figs, brown sugar, salt, and pepper to the pan. Simmer 10 to 15 minutes, until the pork chops are just tender. Remove the pork chops and keep warm. Gently simmer to reduce the sauce, about 10 minutes longer. Pour the sauce over the pork chops.

If Rhino Chasers® American Amber Ale is not available, see Substitution Chart.

SPICY DORMUNDER GOLD BASTED HAM

24 OR MORE SERVINGS

A Tavern Ham is boneless, and delightfully smoky. When there is a crowd to please, from a cocktail buffet to a summer picnic, this recipe is sure to be a favorite. Serve it with Onion Marmalade (page 163) for a bit of welcomed tartness.

I	cup light brown sugar, *packed*
I	cup Dijon mustard
I	tablespoon ground allspice
I	(12- to 14-pound) Tavern or other fully-cooked ham
2	cups water
I	cup Great Lakes® Dortmunder Gold beer

Preheat the oven to 350°F. Combine the brown sugar, mustard, and allspice in a medium bowl, then set aside. Place the ham on a rack in a large roasting pan. Brush well with the mustard-sugar mixture. Add the water and beer to the bottom of the roasting pan.

Roast 12 minutes a pound (approximately 2 hours and 20 minutes) or until the internal temperature of the ham reaches 140°F. on a meat thermometer. Baste occasionally with the pan juices for the last hour of cooking. Transfer the ham to a large serving platter, slice, and serve. Skim any fat from the pan juices, then pour into a gravy boat. Accompany the ham with Onion Marmalade with Celis Raspberry Beer *(see Headnote)*, mustards, the pan juices, and a cornucopia of breads and rolls.

If Great Lakes® Dortmunder Gold beer is not available, see Substitution Chart.

CORNED BEEF HASH TAMALE
CON CERVESA

6 TAMALES

The best place to get fresh masa, or corn dough, is from a local tortilleria, but if that is not an option here is an easy recipe for making your own.

MASA

1 ½	cups water
¼	cup corn oil
2	cups masa harina
½	teaspoon baking powder
	Salt and freshly ground pepper, to taste

Combine the water and oil in a medium saucepan and bring to a boil. Sift the masa harina through your fingers and into the pot, whisking until smooth. Add the baking powder, salt, and pepper. Continue stirring until the masa is shiny and pulls away from sides of the pot. Set aside to cool.

FILLING

1	pound corned beef
1	tablespoon butter
½	cup diced onion
1	cup diced green bell pepper
3	cloves garlic, *minced*
2	tablespoons flour
1	cup Corona® beer
¼	teaspoon dried thyme
1	tablespoon chopped fresh Italian parsley
1	tablespoon freshly ground pepper
¾	pound potatoes, *baked, peeled, and diced*
6	corn husks

Combine the beef with enough water to cover in a large heavy saucepan. Simmer 1 hour. Remove the beef and boil the liquid in the pan until reduced to ½ cup.

Melt the butter in a skillet over medium heat and sauté the onion, green pepper, and garlic until soft, about 8 minutes. Stir in the flour and cook 1 minute. Pour in the beer and reduced stock and simmer until the sauce thickens. Remove from the heat.

Slice the beef thinly across the grain and then cut to form long strips. Place them in a large bowl with the thyme, parsley, pepper, potatoes, and sauce. Mix well.

To make the tamales, spread 2 tablespoons of masa in the center of each husk, forming a rectangle leaving 1 inch bare on the left and 2 inches bare on the top and bottom. Place 3 tablespoons of beef filling in the center. Enclose by folding first the right and then the left sides over. Fold up the bottom and then the top to close. Tie with a ¼-inch-wide strip of husk (or kitchen string) to secure.

Prepare a large pot with a steamer rack and water. Bring the water to a boil. Stack the tamales loosely, seam side down, on the rack. Cover and steam over medium heat about 35 minutes, or until husks easily pull away from the dough. To serve, unwrap the tamales and place them on a warm platter.

If Corona® beer is not available, see Substitution Chart.

CHEF
G. RICHARD POINTER

LA CASCADA
RESTAURANT/
DOUBLETREE HOTEL
ALBUQUERQUE, NM

TENDERLOIN CHIPOTLE RAGOUT

4 SERVINGS

Here is an elegant beef sauté to serve over hot noodles.
For less heat, just use fewer dried peppers.

3 ½	tablespoons butter
1 ½	pounds beef tenderloin, *cut in ¾-inch-thick slices*
½	pound thinly sliced mushrooms caps
1	medium onion, *finely chopped*
1	(12-ounce) bottle Heineken® beer, plus additional to thin sauce (optional)
1	pint heavy cream
2	tablespoons roux blanc *(see Note)*
3	canned chipotle peppers, *seeded and chopped*
	Salt, to taste
¾	cup sour cream
1/4	cup chopped fresh Italian parsley
	Beef stock, for thinning sauce (optional)
1	pound hot cooked fettuccine

In a large skillet, melt 2 tablespoons of the butter over medium heat. Brown the beef about 2 minutes on each side. Remove the beef and set aside. Add the mushrooms and onion to the skillet and sauté about 7 minutes, adding more butter if needed. Pour in the beer and cook over medium heat, stirring occasionally, until the liquid is reduced by half, about 4 minutes. Add the cream and reduce the liquid by half again, about 8 minutes. Add the roux blanc and cook, stirring, until thickened, about 3 minutes. Stir in the chipotle peppers and salt to taste. Simmer about 3 to 4 minutes. Add the beef just to heat through. Stir in the sour cream and parsley and remove from the heat. (Thin the sauce with a few tablespoons of beef stock or beer if it appears too thick.) Serve over hot fettuccine.

If Heineken® beer is not available, see Substitution Chart.

Note:
To make the roux blanc, in a small skillet heat 1 ½ tablespoons of butter until bubbly. Add 1 ½ tablespoons of all-purpose flour and cook, stirring, until the mixture is foamy, about 1 minute. Makes 2 tablespoons roux blanc.

WILD BOAR STEW WITH PORTER

6 TO 8 SERVINGS

An excellent dish to make in advance, this stew benefits from a day or two in the refrigerator. Serving this dish with small red, herbed potatoes will give it just the right touch.

3	pounds wild boar meat, *cut into 1 ¼-inch pieces (see Note)*
3 to 4	celery ribs, *chopped*
2	medium carrots, *chopped*
1	small onion, *chopped*
2	medium cloves garlic, *minced*
4	bay leaves
1	cinnamon stick
1	tablespoon rock salt
	Freshly ground pepper, to taste
2 ¼	cups Anchor® Steam Porter
3	tablespoons all-purpose flour
6	tablespoons olive oil
1	quart canned tomato puree

Place the meat in a large bowl and cover with the celery, carrots, and onion. Add the garlic, bay leaves, and cinnamon stick. Sprinkle with the salt and pepper. Pour the porter over the meat and vegetables. Cover and marinate in the refrigerator for 24 hours, or longer.

To cook, strain the liquid and reserve. Separate the meat from the vegetable/spice mixture. Pat the meat dry with paper towels and coat it lightly with flour. In a large casserole, over medium-high heat, brown the meat on all sides in 3 tablespoons of the olive oil. Remove the meat and set aside. In the remaining 3 tablespoons of olive oil, sauté the drained vegetable mixture until lightly browned. Return the meat to the pan and cook 5 minutes longer.

Pour in the reserved liquid and bring to a boil. Reduce the heat to medium and boil gently to reduce the liquid by about half, about 15 minutes. Stir in the tomato puree, cover, and simmer about 1 hour, or until the meat is tender. Season with pepper to taste. Remove from the heat and let stand about 2 hours to blend the flavors. Discard the bay leaves and cinnamon stick. Reheat before serving.

If Anchor® Steam Porter is not available, see Substitution Chart.

CHEF
CELESTINO DRAGO

DRAGO RISTORANTE
SANTA MONICA, CA
IL PISTAIO
BEVERLY HILLS
AND
PASADENA, CA

Note:
If you haven't had an encounter with a wild boar lately, pork shoulder (with excess fat removed) or pork tenderloin can be substituted for the wild boar meat. If used, marinate only 4 to 6 hours.

VEAL OSSO BEERCO

6 TO 8 SERVINGS

This wonderful dish for cool winter evenings and the round of holiday parties can be assembled and put in the oven before the guests arrive. It can be combined with Barley Mushroom Pilaf, page 162, or just about anything. Just let your individual fancy guide you.

1	cup all-purpose flour
	Salt and freshly ground pepper, to taste
8	(2-inch-thick) veal shanks
¼	cup extra virgin olive oil
¼	cup unsalted butter
2	large onions, *coarsely chopped*
8	medium cloves garlic, *minced*
½	cup coarsely chopped red bell pepper
1	teaspoon dried oregano leaves
1	(28-ounce) can Italian-style plum tomatoes with basil, *diced and drained*
¼	cup sliced fresh basil leaves
1	cup Rhino Chasers® American Amber Ale
1	tablespoon fresh lemon juice
1	tablespoon maple syrup
¼	teaspoon malt vinegar
5	cups beef stock or broth
½	cup chopped fresh Italian parsley, for garnish

Preheat the oven to 350°F. In a plastic or paper bag, combine the flour, salt, and pepper. Add a few veal shanks at a time and coat well with flour, shaking off any excess. In a large Dutch oven, heat the olive oil and butter over medium to high heat. Briefly brown the veal on all sides. Remove and set aside.

Adding more olive oil if necessary, sauté the onions, garlic, red pepper, and oregano, stirring occasionally, until the vegetables are soft, about 10 minutes. Add the diced tomatoes, the basil, and salt and pepper to taste. Simmer, uncovered for 5 minutes. Add the ale, lemon juice, maple syrup, and vinegar and cook 10 minutes longer. Return the veal shanks to the pot and add enough of the stock just to cover. Bake, covered, in the preheated oven for 1 ½ hours. Uncover and bake until the veal is tender, about 30 minutes longer. To serve, pour some of the tomato sauce over the veal and sprinkle with the parsley. Pour the remaining sauce in a gravy bowl and serve on the side.

If Rhino Chasers® American Amber Ale is not available, see Substitution Chart.

BOB'S BOEUF BEERGUIGNON

6 SERVINGS

This satisfying entree is excellent served with fluffy rice.

1	large eggplant, *unpeeled, cut into 1-inch cubes*
2	tablespoons salt
2	tablespoons all-purpose flour
2	tablespoons dry mustard
1	teaspoon freshly ground pepper
2	pounds boneless sirloin or other lean beef, *cut into 1-inch cubes*
2	tablespoons vegetable oil
6	medium cloves garlic
6	tablespoons butter
3	medium onions, *thinly sliced*
¾	pound fresh porcini or oyster mushrooms, *cut into large pieces* (about 4 cups)
1	(12-ounce) bottle Rhino Chasers® American Amber Ale
1 ½	cups beef stock or broth
1	tablespoon chopped fresh basil leaves
2	bay leaves

In a large bowl, soak the eggplant in water to cover with 1 tablespoon salt for ½ to 1 hour.

In a shallow bowl, combine the flour, dry mustard, and pepper. Roll the beef in the flour mixture and set aside. In a large skillet, heat the oil over medium-high heat and sauté the garlic until lightly brown. Remove the garlic and set aside. Add the beef and brown it on all sides over medium to high heat, stirring frequently. Remove the beef cubes and reserve with the garlic.

To the same skillet, add 2 tablespoons of the butter and sauté the onions over medium heat until soft and lightly browned, about 10 minutes. Remove the onions and reserve with the beef.

Add 2 more tablespoons of butter and sauté the mushrooms with 1 teaspoon of salt over medium heat, until they start to give up their liquid and are lightly browned, about 5 minutes. Remove the mushrooms and reserve with the beef.

Drain the eggplant well and pat it dry with paper towels. In a large saucepot, sauté the eggplant over medium heat with 1 teaspoon of salt, in the remaining 2 tablespoons of butter. Add 2 tablespoons of the ale and cook, stirring frequently, until the eggplant starts to soften, about 7 minutes. Return the reserved garlic cloves, beef, onions, and mushrooms and mix well. Pour in the remaining ale, the beef stock, basil, bay leaves, and 1 teaspoon salt. Bring to a boil. Reduce the heat to a simmer and cook, covered, for 1 ½ to 2 hours or until the beef is tender. Stir occasionally and add more ale or stock if necessary to keep the beef moist. Remove and discard the bay leaves before serving.

If Rhino Chasers® American Amber Ale is not available, see Substitution Chart.

FLANK STEAK WITH
SPICY BEER MARINADE

8 TO 12 SERVINGS

Serve with roasted corn on the cob, a tossed green salad,
hot garlic bread, and your favorite beer.

4	pounds beef flank steak
1	(12-ounce) bottle Full Sail® American Amber Ale
½	cup olive oil
½	cup soy sauce
½	cup canned tomato sauce or ketchup
¼	cup Worcestershire sauce
½	bunch cilantro leaves, *chopped*
1	(2-inch) piece fresh ginger, *finely chopped*
3	cloves garlic, *minced*
1	tablespoon cracked black pepper
1	teaspoon crushed dried red pepper, or 1 fresh jalapeño pepper, *finely diced*

With a knife, score the surface of the steak on both sides in a diamond pattern. Place it in a glass dish just large enough to hold it. In a medium bowl, whisk together the remaining ingredients and pour the marinade over the steak. Cover and marinate in the refrigerator for 2 to 4 hours.

To cook, preheat a grill or barbecue. Remove the steak from the marinade and grill or barbecue over glowing coals or medium-high heat for 4 to 6 minutes per side, or longer to taste, brushing it occasionally with the marinade.

If Full Sail® American Amber Ale is not available, see Substitution Chart.

SPICY BRAISED SHORT RIBS

4 SERVINGS

A multitude of flavors are blended to create these short ribs with a Southeast Asian accent.

CHEF
SCOTT BRYAN
∾
LUMA RESTAURANT
NEW YORK, NY

2	tablespoons whole black peppercorns
2	tablespoons coriander seeds
2	star anise
4	green cardamom pods
	Salt, to taste
4 to 4 ½	pounds beef short ribs, *cut across ribs into 2-inch pieces*
1/3	cup vegetable oil
3	tablespoons butter
2	medium onions, *diced*
2	medium carrots, *diced*
2	celery ribs, *diced*
3 to 4	tablespoons minced fresh ginger
¼	cup minced fresh lemongrass *(see Note)*
1	tablespoon minced garlic
5	fresh or dried kaffir lime leaves, *minced* (optional)
1	quart Anderson Valley® Stout
2	cups beef stock or broth
2	large tomatoes, *chopped*
	Juice and zest of 1 large orange
2	tablespoons soy sauce
1 ½	tablespoons hoisin sauce

Combine the black pepper, coriander, star anise, and cardamoms in a spice grinder. Grind to medium fine. Lightly salt the short ribs and rub the spice mixture all over the ribs. Set aside

Note: Lemongrass and kaffir lime leaves can be found in Thai, Vietnamese, and some other Asian markets.

at room temperature for 1 hour.

Preheat the oven to 375°F. In an ovenproof saucepot or Dutch oven, heat the oil over medium-high heat, and brown the ribs on all sides. Remove the ribs and set aside.

Melt the butter and sauté the onions, carrots, and celery over medium heat until the vegetables are soft, about 10 minutes. Add the ginger, lemongrass, garlic, and kaffir lime leaves and sauté 2 to 3 minutes longer. Pour in the stout, beef stock, tomatoes, orange zest and juice, and the soy and hoisin sauces. Stir well. Return the short ribs to the pot and stir to mix well. Cover and bake in the preheated oven for 2 hours, until the short ribs are fork-tender. (Uncover and cook ½ hour longer if necessary.) Serve with horseradish, mashed potatoes, and douse the ribs with the remaining broth.

If Anderson Valley® Stout is not available, see Substitution Chart.

VENISON CHOPS WITH
BEER—POACHED PEARS

4 SERVINGS

CHEF
JOSIE LeBALCH

SADDLE PEAK LODGE
CALABASAS, CA

Ask your butcher for New Zealand venison if you are new to the cooking game. It has a milder flavor than wild venison and does not require tenderizing. Offset the darkness of this combination with some colorful vegetables such as sautéed corn, wilted bitter greens or red chard.

VENISON

3	(12-ounce) bottles Rhino Chasers® American Amber Ale
3	tablespoons brown sugar
1	cinnamon stick
3	tablespoons lemon juice and rind
4	small firm pears, *peeled with stems on*
12	ounces reserved pear poaching liquid
2	cups veal stock
1	tablespoon lingonberries
1	tablespoon butter
4	(8-ounce) venison chops
2	tablespoons olive oil
	Salt and freshly ground pepper, to taste

Combine the ale, sugar, cinnamon, and the lemon juice and rind in a medium saucepan. Using a small melon baller, core the pears and discard ½-inch of the bottom. Place the pears in the beer mixture, adding more beer if necessary to cover. Simmer until a toothpick can easily be inserted, being careful not to overcook. Remove the pears and transfer them to the refrigerator. Reserve the poaching liquid.

To make the sauce, remove and discard the cinnamon stick. Bring the liquid to a boil and reduce it to one-third, about 15 minutes. Add the veal stock and reduce it by one-third, about 5 minutes. Remove the sauce from the heat and stir in the lingonberries and butter, if desired. Keep warm.

Preheat the oven to 425°F. Season the chops generously with salt and pepper. Heat the olive oil over high heat in a large ovenproof skillet. Cook the chops about

4 minutes per side. Transfer them to the oven and bake about 5 minutes to cook through, being careful not to overcook since venison toughens considerably as it cooks. Place each chop on a plate, along with a cold pear. Spoon the sauce over the meat and serve.

If Rhino Chasers® American Amber Ale is not available, see Substitution Chart.

VENISON CHILI WITH BLACK BEANS

6 SERVINGS

This is a long recipe, but it is easily handled in stages. Chicken or beef stock maybe substituted for the venison stock.

VENISON

1	(4-pound) venison shoulder or leg, with bone (*see Note*)
2	teaspoons chili powder
½	teaspoon crushed red pepper
¼	teaspoon each dried oregano and dried thyme leaves, *crushed*
¼	teaspoon each ground cumin and ground coriander
⅛	teaspoon cayenne pepper
1	(12-ounce) bottle Rhino Chasers® Dark Roasted Läger beer
7	medium cloves garlic, *crushed*
2	bay leaves
1	small bunch cilantro
8	sprigs fresh Italian parsley with stems

Bone the venison and trim off any excess fat, saving both fat and bones for making the venison stock, if desired (see below). Cut the venison into ¾-inch cubes to yield 1 ½ to 2 pounds meat cubes.

In a large bowl, combine the chili powder, crushed red pepper, oregano, thyme, cumin, coriander, and cayenne. Add the cubed venison and toss to coat the meat evenly. Add the beer, garlic, and bay leaves. Tie the cilantro and parsley together with kitchen twine and add it to the mixture. Mix well, cover, and marinate in the refrigerator for 24 hours, stirring occasionally.

CHILI

3	thick slices bacon
2	medium onions, *chopped*
5	medium cloves garlic, *minced*
3	cups Venison Stock (see below), or chicken or beef stock
3	smoked ham hocks

CHEF
. BRADLEY OGDEN

THE LARK CREEK INN
LARKSPUR, CA
ONE MARKET
SAN FRANCISCO, CA

*Note:
If you do not make the venison stock, start with 2 pounds boneless venison shoulder or leg and cut into ¾-inch cubes.*

1	cup dried black beans, *presoaked overnight*
1	cup chopped Roma (Italian plum) tomatoes or tomato juice
¼	cup finely chopped Anaheim chiles, with seeds
½	ounce unsweetened chocolate, *chopped*
2	teaspoons chili powder
½	teaspoon ground cumin
	Dash of cayenne pepper
	Reserved marinated venison
1 to 2	tablespoons olive oil
	Crème fraîche or sour cream, for garnish (optional)

In a large saucepot over medium heat, fry the bacon until crisp, stirring occasionally. Add the onions and sauté 2 minutes; add the garlic and sauté 2 minutes longer. Add the stock, ham hocks, drained presoaked beans, tomatoes or juice, chiles, chocolate, chili powder, cumin, and cayenne. Bring to a boil, reduce the heat to a simmer, and cook, covered, for 45 minutes.

While the chili simmers, remove the meat from the marinade and pat dry. Discard the marinade. Heat the olive oil in a large skillet and brown the meat on all sides over medium-high heat. Add the meat to the chili and simmer, uncovered, for 1 hour, or until the meat and beans are very tender. Add additional stock as necessary. Remove the ham hocks and cool slightly. Pull the meat from the hocks and return it to the pot. Ladle the chili into bowls and top it with dollops of crème fraîche or sour cream, if desired.

VENISON STOCK

2	pounds fat, bones and trimmings from 4-pound venison shoulder or leg
3	celery ribs, *quartered*
2	medium carrots, *quartered*
1	medium onion, *cut into wedges*
1	head garlic, *unpeeled, cut in half crosswise*
1	(28-ounce) can Italian-style plum tomatoes with basil, *undrained*
1	(12-ounce) bottle Rhino Chasers® Dark Roasted Läger beer
2	tablespoons red wine vinegar
1	Anaheim chile, *cut in half*
10	fresh Italian parsley sprigs
6	sprigs fresh thyme
1	bay leaf

1 ½	teaspoons chili powder
½	teaspoon crushed red pepper
¼	teaspoon ground cumin

Preheat the oven to 425°F. Render the venison fat by melting it in a flameproof roasting pan over medium heat. Add the bones and trimmings and stir to coat evenly. Place the pan in the oven and roast, uncovered, stirring often for 30 minutes, or until the bones are brown. Remove from the oven and add the celery, carrots, onion, and garlic. Roast until lightly browned and caramelized, about 10 minutes longer. Remove from the oven and place the bones and vegetables in a large saucepot, discarding the fat.

Add a small amount of water to the roasting pan. Heat briefly, stirring to loosen any brown bits, and pour the contents of the pan into the saucepot. Add all the remaining ingredients and 2 quarts of water and bring to a boil, stirring occasionally. Reduce the heat and simmer 2 hours, skimming the foam occasionally. Strain through a cheesecloth-lined sieve or colander, pressing out the solids with the back of a large spoon. Refrigerate the stock and discard the congealed fat that rises to the top. Any extra stock can be frozen for future use, in a clean glass jar (leaving ½-inch from the top to allow for the frozen stock to expand), approximately 2 months.

If Rhino Chasers® Dark Roasted Läger beer is not available, see Substitution Chart.

Side Dishes

*Beer can be used to add interest
to a wide variety of vegetables and side dishes. Rice steamed with beer
rather than water has a distinctive and agreeable flavor that
goes well with many dishes.
Potatoes boiled in beer are a good way of enhancing a potato salad, which
can further benefit from a dash of stout or porter in the dressing.
A good amber lager supplies character and robustness to
Boston baked beans, and almost any sweet vegetable will acquire a new
accent from being cooked with beer, as will other side dishes such as
dumplings or Yorkshire pudding.*

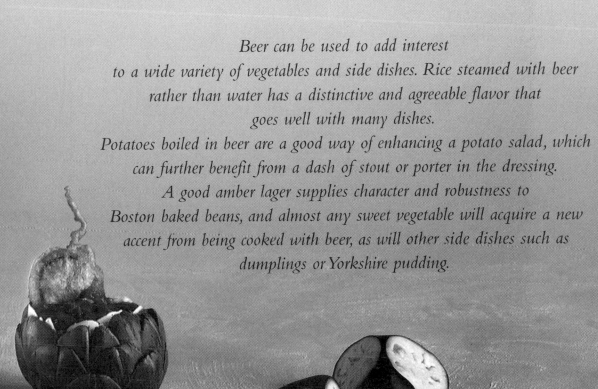

CHEFS
"ALASKAN BREW
CREW"

ALASKAN BREWING
COMPANY
JUNEAU, AK

AUTUMN APPLE—POTATO GRATIN

6 SERVINGS

Your guests will wonder what gives this potato gratin its distinctive flavor. Yukon Gold potatoes have a butter-yellow color and moist texture. It is sure to be part of your repertoire.

4	tablespoons all-purpose flour
2	teaspoons salt
1	teaspoon freshly ground white pepper
1	teaspoon dried thyme, *crushed*
¼	teaspoon cayenne pepper
1 ½	pounds Yukon Gold potatoes, *peeled and thinly sliced (see Note)*
5	tablespoons butter, *melted and slightly cooled*
4 to 5	medium green-skinned apples, *peeled, cored, and thinly sliced*
2	medium onions, *thinly sliced*
1	(12-ounce) bottle Alaskan® Autumn Ale
1	cup heavy cream
2	large cloves garlic, *minced*
⅔	cup grated Swiss cheese
¼	teaspoon dried rosemary, *crushed*

Preheat the oven to 375°F. Butter a 12 x 8 x 2-inch baking dish. In a small bowl, stir together the flour, salt, white pepper, thyme, and cayenne. Toss the potatoes with half the melted butter. Toss the apples with the remaining butter.

Layer half the potatoes in the prepared baking dish. Sprinkle with one fourth of the flour mixture. Layer half the apples and onions over the potatoes. Sprinkle with one fourth of the flour mixture. Repeat the layers, sprinkling flour in between. Combine the ale, cream, and garlic and pour over the top. Cover and bake 45 minutes. Reduce the oven temperature to 350°F., uncover the casserole, and bake 15 minutes longer. Sprinkle with the cheese and rosemary. Bake until the cheese melts, about 5 minutes longer.

❖

If Alaskan® Autumn Ale is not available, see Substitution Chart.

FOURTH OF JULY POTATO SALAD

6 TO 8 SERVINGS

TAMARA THOMAS

PRESIDENT,
FINE ARTS SERVICES, INC.
LOS ANGELES, CA

Don't be misled, this tasty potato salad is a year-round favorite.

2	pounds medium red potatoes, *unpeeled*
5	tablespoons cider vinegar
2	teaspoons Dijon mustard
1	teaspoon salt
	Freshly ground pepper, to taste
4	slices bacon
1	large red onion, *chopped* (about 2 cups)
2	tablespoons vegetable oil
½	cup Rhino Chasers® American Amber Ale
¼	cup finely diced red bell pepper

Boil the potatoes in water to cover until just tender, 20 to 30 minutes. Drain and let the potatoes cool. When cool enough to handle, peel and cut them in half. Cut the potato halves into ¼-inch-thick slices and place them in a large bowl. Combine 3 tablespoons of the vinegar, the mustard, and salt and pepper to taste. Pour the mixture over the warm sliced potatoes and toss lightly.

In a skillet, fry the bacon until crisp. Remove and drain the bacon, reserving the drippings in the skillet. Crumble the bacon over the potatoes. In the reserved bacon drippings, sauté the onion over medium heat until just tender, adding vegetable oil as needed to prevent the onions from sticking to the skillet. Pour in the ale and the remaining vinegar. Heat just to deglaze the skillet, stirring to loosen any browned bits. Pour the ale-onion mixture over the potatoes. Add the red pepper and toss well. Serve at room temperature.

If Rhino Chasers® American Amber Ale is not available, see Substitution Chart.

LEEK AND PALE ALE TART

8 TO 10 SERVINGS

Leeks are a mild onion, made even milder by slow cooking.

	Tart pastry for 1 (12-inch) tart pan (see below)
6	large leeks, *cleaned and chopped (see Note)*
2	tablespoons olive oil
¾	cup Samuel Smith® Pale Ale
2	eggs
⅔	cup light cream or half and half
½	cup freshly grated Romano cheese
4	ounces Italian fontina cheese, *grated or sliced*
	Freshly ground pepper, to taste

Prick the bottom of the pastry with a fork. Bake at 425°F. for 5 to 8 minutes to partially cook but not brown the pastry. Remove from the oven and set aside. Turn the oven down to 350°F.

In a large skillet, sauté the leeks in the oil, stirring constantly over medium heat, until they start to wilt. Add ½ cup of the ale and continue cooking until the leeks are limp and the ale is nearly absorbed.

In a small bowl, whisk together the eggs, cream, and the remaining ¼ cup ale. Sprinkle the Romano cheese into the prebaked tart shell. Add the leeks. Pour the egg mixture over the leeks and sprinkle the top with the fontina cheese and pepper to taste. Bake 35 to 45 minutes, or until a knife inserted in the center comes out clean.

TART PASTRY - Makes 1 (12-inch) tart shell

2	cups all-purpose flour
½	teaspoon salt
½	cup (1 stick) unsalted butter, *cut into small pieces*
¼	cup vegetable shortening, *chilled in freezer*
5 to 7	tablespoons ice water

In a large bowl, stir together the flour and salt. With a pastry blender, cut in the butter and shortening until the pieces are the size of small peas. Add 5 tablespoons of ice water, tossing the mixture with a fork to incorporate just enough moisture so that the dough can be formed

Note:

To prepare the leeks, trim the roots and dark upper leaves to about 1 ½ inches above the white part and discard. Cut the leeks in half lengthwise and soak or rinse well in cold water to remove any sand between the leaves.

into a ball. If dough is dry, add more ice water one teaspoonful at a time. Flatten into a disc, wrap it in plastic, and chill for 1 hour. Let the dough soften slightly at room temperature before rolling. Flatten the dough on a lightly floured board and roll it out to a 14-inch circle. Line a 12-inch tart pan with the pastry.

If Samuel Smith® Pale Ale is not available, see Substitution Chart.

B. J. DOERFLING

FOOD WRITER

AND

CONSULTANT

AGOURA HILLS, CA

BARLEY MUSHROOM PILAF

6 SERVINGS

This hearty accompaniment goes well with grilled lamb or beef.

1	medium onion, *diced*
5	ounces mushrooms, *cut in half and sliced*
4	tablespoons butter
1 ¼	cups pearl barley
1 ½	cups chicken stock or broth
1	cup Rhino Chasers® Lager beer
⅓	cup diced red or green bell pepper
⅛	teaspoon salt
½	teaspoon freshly ground white pepper
⅓	cup coarsely chopped roasted cashew nuts

In a large skillet, sauté the mushrooms over medium to high heat in 2 tablespoons of the butter, for about 2 minutes. In another large heavy saucepan over medium heat, sauté the barley and onion in the remaining 2 tablespoons of the butter until the barley is lightly toasted. Add the mushrooms to the barley-onion mixture. Add the chicken stock, beer, red pepper, salt, and pepper and bring to a boil. Reduce the heat, cover, and simmer for 50 to 60 minutes, or until the barley is just tender and almost all the liquid is absorbed. Fluff with a fork, gently stir in the nuts, and serve.

If Rhino Chasers® Lager beer is not available, see Substitution Chart.

KILLER MEXICAN RICE

6 TO 8 SERVINGS

CHEF
BRUCE AIDELLS

AIDELLS SAUSAGE
COMPANY
SAN LEANDRO, CA

This version of Mexican rice is light, fluffy, and packed with flavor.

2	tablespoons olive oil
½	Mexican chorizo sausage, removed from the casing (optional)
1	large onion, *finely chopped*
½	cup finely chopped carrots
1	tablespoon chopped garlic
2	cups long grain rice
1	tablespoon chili powder
2	cups chicken stock or broth
1	cup Mexican beer such as Modelo® Negro or Bohemia®
¾	cup canned tomato sauce
2	Anaheim chiles, *roasted, seeded, and chopped,* or 2 canned whole green chiles, *chopped*
	Salt and freshly ground pepper, to taste

In a heavy 2-quart saucepan, heat the oil over medium heat. Add the sausage, if desired, and the onion and sauté 10 minutes, until the onion is soft. Add the carrots and garlic and sauté 2 minutes longer. Add the rice and chili powder and stir until the rice is well coated. Pour in the chicken stock, beer, tomato sauce, chiles, and salt and pepper to taste. Bring to a boil, reduce the heat to a simmer, cover, and cook 20 to 25 minutes. Let sit 5 minutes, fluff the rice with a fork, and serve.

If Modelo® Negro or Bohemia® beer is not available, see Substitution Chart.

CARAWAY—SCENTED RED CABBAGE BRAISED IN ALE

6 SERVINGS

If you're looking for a meatless vegetable accompaniment, this cabbage dish has exceptional flavor even without the sausage.

I	medium head red cabbage, *cored and coarsely chopped*
I	(12-ounce) bottle Red Tail® Ale
2	teaspoons salt
½	teaspoon caraway seeds
I	tablespoon cooking oil
I	large onion, *chopped*
I	tablespoon sugar
2	Granny Smith apples, *cored, peeled, and cut into ½-inch cubes* (about 3 cups)
I	pound smoked kielbasa sausage, *cut lengthwise, then crosswise into ½-inch slices*
I	tablespoon malt or cider vinegar

In a large saucepot, combine the cabbage, ale, salt, and caraway seeds. Bring to a boil. Reduce the heat, cover, and simmer 30 minutes. Uncover and continue cooking until most of the liquid has evaporated, about 10 to 15 minutes. Set aside and reserve.

In a large skillet, heat the oil over medium heat. Add the onion and cook, stirring frequently, until the onion is golden, about 6 minutes. Add the sugar and cook until the onion is slightly caramelized. Stir in the apples and cook 5 minutes longer. Add the sausage and vinegar and sauté for 5 minutes. Add the apple-sausage mixture to the cabbage in the saucepot, stirring well. Cover and simmer to blend the flavors, about 20 minutes.

If Red Tail® Ale is not available, see Substitution Chart.

ONION MARMALADE WITH
CELIS RASPBERRY BEER

MAKES ABOUT 2 CUPS

*Serve this savory marmalade with Spicy Dormunder
Gold Basted Ham (page 137).*

1	tablespoon extra-virgin olive oil
1	pound onions, *diced*
1	tablespoon all-purpose flour
1	cup sugar
¾	cup Celis® Raspberry beer
½	cup red wine vinegar
4	sprigs fresh thyme
8	whole cloves
1	bay leaf
	Salt and freshly ground pepper, to taste

Heat the olive oil in a large, heavy skillet and sauté the onions over medium-low heat until soft and transparent, about 7 minutes. Stir in the flour and blend well. Add the remaining ingredients and bring to a boil, stirring occasionally. Reduce the heat, cover, and simmer 45 minutes. Remove from the heat and discard the thyme sprigs, cloves, and bay leaf. Cool the onions and pour them into a container with a tight-fitting lid. The marmalade will keep in the refrigerator for several weeks.

If Celis® Raspberry beer is not available, see Substitution Chart.

CHEF
MARIE–CLAIRE
QUITTELIER

BELGIAN TRADING
COMPANY
AUSTIN, TX

CHEF
JAMES D. THOMPSON

HOTEL MEXICO
CINCINNATI, OH

GRILLED PORTOBELLO MUSHROOMS

2 SERVINGS

Portobello mushrooms, when grilled, make an excellent change-of-pace side dish, or they can be used to create a deluxe sandwich, served on sourdough bread.

½	cup Rhino Chasers® Lager beer
2	tablespoons olive oil
I	tablespoon minced garlic
	Salt and freshly ground pepper, to taste
2	portobello mushrooms, *stems removed*

In a medium bowl, whisk together the beer, olive oil, garlic, salt, and pepper. Add the mushrooms to the marinade. Cover and marinate in the refrigerator for 2 hours.

Preheat a grill, barbecue, or broiler. Remove the mushrooms from the marinade and grill, barbecue, or broil them for about 5 minutes on each side.

If Rhino Chasers® Lager beer is not available, see Substitution Chart.

JAPANESE EGGPLANT WITH CAYENNE BEER BATTER AND SPICY ROASTED BELL PEPPER DIP

12 TO 16 SERVINGS

Spicy, crispy, and utterly delicious.

CHEF
FAZ POURSOHI

FAZ RESTAURANTS
AND
CATERING
SAN FRANCISCO, CA

BATTER

4	eggs
1	(12-ounce) bottle Rhino Chasers® Lager beer
1 ½	cups all-purpose flour
2	tablespoons baking powder
2	teaspoons freshly grated lemon peel
1	teaspoon cayenne pepper
1	teaspoon paprika

3	pounds Japanese eggplant, *unpeeled, cut into ¾- to 1-inch-thick slices*
½	cup olive oil
	Salt and freshly ground pepper, to taste
	Vegetable oil, for deep frying (about 2 quarts)
1 to 1 ½	cups all-purpose flour
½	cup freshly grated Parmesan cheese
½	cup chopped fresh Italian parsley
	Spicy Roasted Bell Pepper Dip (see following page)

In a large bowl, lightly beat the eggs with a whisk. Add the remaining ingredients and beat until the batter is smooth. Cover with plastic wrap and set aside at room temperature for 30 minutes or longer.

Preheat the oven to 350°F. Brush the eggplant with the olive oil and sprinkle it with salt and pepper. Place it in a single layer on a baking sheet and bake in the preheated oven for 10 to 12 minutes, or until just tender. Remove from the oven and cool. In a deep-fryer, heat the vegetable oil to 375°F. Dip a few of the eggplant slices into the flour to coat lightly, then dip into the batter, coating well. Carefully slip the eggplant into the heated oil and deep-fry until golden brown, turning with a fork to brown all sides. Remove the fried eggplant and drain on paper towels. Keep warm while preparing the remaining eggplant. Serve in napkin-lined baskets, sprinkled with the Parmesan cheese and parsley, and accompanied by the spicy roasted bell pepper dip.

SPICY ROASTED BELL PEPPER DIP – Makes ¾ cup

3	large red bell peppers
4	Roma (Italian plum) tomatoes
1/4	cup plus 2 tablespoons olive oil
1/8	teaspoon crushed red pepper
	Salt and freshly ground pepper, to taste

Preheat the oven to 450°F. or preheat a grill or gas barbecue. Rub the peppers and tomatoes with 2 tablespoons of the olive oil. Roast the peppers and tomatoes in a baking pan, turning often until charred on all sides, about 10 to 20 minutes. As the vegetables are charred, remove and place them in a plastic bag to steam and to loosen the skins. When cool enough to handle, rub off the blackened skins (do not rinse under water) and remove the cores and seeds. Cut the peppers into large pieces and place them in a food processor or blender. Add the remaining olive oil and the crushed red pepper; blend until smooth. Season with salt and pepper.

If Rhino Chasers® Lager beer is not available, see Substitution Chart.

ROBERT'S SEASONAL
FLORAL DELIGHT

4 TO 6 SERVINGS

ROBERT DORNHELM

FILM DIRECTOR
NEW YORK, NY

This dish calls for blooming zucchini blossoms (see Headnote, page 164).

2	eggs
½	cup flour
3 to 6	tablespoons Rhino Chasers® Lager beer
1/2	teaspoon salt, or to taste
	Freshly ground pepper, to taste
18	zucchini or squash blossoms, *stamens and stems removed*
3	ounces Swiss Emmentaler and/or goat cheese, *grated or finely chopped*
2	ounces thinly sliced prosciutto or ham
2	tablespoons olive oil, or more as needed
2	tablespoons vegetable oil, or more as needed

In a medium bowl, lightly beat the eggs and gradually stir in the flour with a fork (the mixture will be quite thick). Gradually stir in just enough beer to form the batter the consistency of pancake batter. Season with salt and pepper and set aside.

Fill the blossoms with cheese and ham, mixing the flavor combinations, as desired. Twist the ends of the flowers to seal in the filling. Heat the oils in a large skillet over medium to high heat.

With a pair of tongs, dip the flowers into the batter and carefully place them in the hot oil, taking care not to crowd the skillet. Lightly brown the blossoms on both sides, about 1 ½ to 2 minutes on each side. Drain them on paper towels, salt to taste, and serve immediately.

If Rhino Chasers® Lager beer is not available, see Substitution Chart.

ZUCCHINI BLOSSOM FRITTERS WITH SWEET AND SOUR SAUCE

4 SERVINGS

Zucchini blossoms are available at farmers' markets in the summertime. They carry the vegetable's essence in their delicate petals.

1 ½	medium red bell peppers, *halved, cored, stemmed, and seeded*
1	Granny Smith apple, *peeled, cored, and diced*
½	cup sugar
5	tablespoons raspberry vinegar
3	eggs, *separated*
½	cup flour
	Salt
¼	cup Celis® White beer
¼	cup olive oil, or more as needed
16	zucchini or other squash blossoms

To make the sauce, place the bell pepper halves in a saucepan of boiling water and boil 3 to 4 minutes. Drain the peppers and, when cool enough to handle, peel and cut them into small cubes. In the same saucepan, combine the peppers, apple, sugar, ½ cup water, and vinegar and bring to a boil. Reduce the heat to a simmer and cook, covered, for 10 minutes, stirring occasionally. Cool slightly, then puree until smooth in a blender or food processor. Strain and return to the saucepan. Reheat before serving, and if the sauce is too thick, thin it with a small amount of water.

To make the fritters, in a large bowl, lightly beat the egg yolks. Stir in the flour and a dash of salt. Gradually whisk in the beer until well blended. In a medium bowl, with an electric or rotary mixer, beat the egg whites with a dash of salt until soft peaks form. Gradually fold the egg whites into the yolk mixture.

Heat the oil in a large skillet over medium to high heat. With a pair of tongs, dip the blossoms into the batter and carefully place them in the hot oil, being careful not to crowd the skillet. Lightly brown the blossoms on both sides, about 2 minutes per side. Drain on paper towels and sprinkle lightly with salt. To serve, spoon 2 to 3 tablespoons of the warm sauce on each plate and top with four of the fritters.

If Celis® White beer is not available, see Substitution Chart.

ALBERTA'S SOUTHERN—STYLE
SPAGHETTI SAUCE

MAKES ABOUT 1 ½ QUARTS, 6 TO 8 SERVINGS

This sauce cooks quickly and the vegetables retain their crunch.

½	cup olive oil
1	large onion, *chopped*
1	large green bell pepper, *cored, seeded, and chopped*
3	medium cloves garlic, *minced*
1	teaspoon dried oregano leaves, *crushed*
1 ½	pounds lean ground beef
1	cup Rhino Chasers® American Amber Ale
¼	pound prosciutto, *chopped*
½	cup tomato paste
2	large tomatoes, *chopped* (about 2 cups with juice)
2	teaspoons salt
½	teaspoon freshly ground pepper
¼	cup each freshly grated Parmesan and Romano cheese

Heat the olive oil in a large saucepot. Sauté the onion, green pepper, garlic, and oregano over medium heat until just tender. Add the beef and brown lightly, stirring occasionally. Add the ale and prosciutto. Stir in the tomato paste. Add the tomatoes and their juice, the salt, pepper, and the cheeses. Bring to a boil, reduce the heat to a simmer, and cook, uncovered, for 10 to 15 minutes.

If Rhino Chasers® American Amber Ale is not available, see Substitution Chart.

CHEF
ALBERTA WRIGHT

JEZEBEL
NEW YORK, NY

EXECUTIVE CHEF
MAURIZIO MAZZON

IL FORNAIO
RESTAURANTS
AND BAKERIES
BEVERLY HILLS,
BURLINGAME,
COSTA MESA,
DEL MAR,
IRVINE,
PALO ALTO,
PASADENA,
SAN FRANCISCO,
SAN JOSE,
AND
SACRAMENTO, CA

RISOTTO ALLA BIERA MORETTI

6 SERVINGS

The test of a good risotto is that it moves like "small waves in the sea" when shaken. If the risotto is too stiff, more broth should be added. Serve alongside garlic-roasted chicken.

1	pound sweet Italian sausage
2	tablespoons olive oil
3	tablespoons minced onion
1	teaspoon minced garlic
1 1/2	cups Moretti® beer
1/2	cup each, roasted and julienned sweet red and yellow bell pepper
3/4	pound Arborio rice
5 to 6	cups chicken broth
1/2	cup freshly grated Parmesan cheese
3 to 4	tablespoons butter
	Salt and freshly ground pepper, to taste

Remove the casings from the sausage. In a large, heavy saucepan, sauté the sausage in the olive oil over medium to high heat until brown and crispy, stirring to break it up into bite-size pieces. Pour off any excess fat from the pan, add the onion and garlic, and sauté over medium heat for 2 to 3 minutes. Pour in the beer and boil gently to reduce by about half. Stir in the peppers and rice and cook for 1 minute longer. Add about 1 cup of the chicken broth, bring back to a gentle boil, and cook, stirring constantly, and adding the broth 1 cup at a time, for about 20 minutes, or until the rice is al dente. Remove from the heat and stir in the Parmesan cheese and butter. Season with salt and pepper to taste *(see Note)*.

If Moretti® beer is not available, see Substitution Chart.

Note:
Serve on warm shallow plates. If the plate is too hot. the risotto will continue to cook, resulting in an "overdone" risotto.

RISOTTO WITH BEER AND WHITE PEACHES

4 SERVINGS

The delicacy of the peaches and wheat beer (and the absence of cheese) make this an exceptionally light risotto. White peaches are a seasonal fruit, available at supermarkets during spring and summertime.

CHEF
FRANCESCO
ANTONUCCI

REMI
NEW YORK, NY
SANTA MONICA, CA
MEXICO CITY,
AND
TEL AVIV, ISRAEL

3	large white peaches
6	tablespoons butter
½	cup diced onion
1 ½	cups Arborio rice
2	cups vegetable stock, *heated*
½	cup dry white wine
½	cup Ayinger® Brau-Weisse beer
	Salt, to taste
1	tablespoon finely chopped fresh mint, for garnish

Bring 2 quarts of water to a boil in a medium saucepan. Blanch the peaches for 30 seconds, drain, and cool. Peel, pit, and reserve 1 peach half. Finely chop the remaining peaches and set aside.

In a large heavy saucepan, melt 4 tablespoons of the butter over medium-low heat, add the onion and cook until it is transparent. Add the rice and stir to coat evenly. Cook, stirring frequently, until it begins to whiten, about 5 minutes. Pour in 2 ladlefuls of hot stock and the wine and cook, stirring frequently, for 3 minutes.

Adjust the heat under the risotto so the liquid keeps bubbling and stir constantly, adding hot stock by the ladleful, until it is nearly all absorbed and the rice is still a bit hard in the middle, about 15 minutes total.

Stir in the chopped peaches and the remaining stock. The rice should be plump and the broth thick. Stir in the beer, and the remaining butter, and season to taste with salt. Remove from heat.

Finely slice the reserved peach half. Place the slices atop the finished risotto, garnish with mint, and serve.

If Ayinger® Brau-Weisse beer is not available, see Substitution Chart.

Breads, Cakes & Desserts

Beer and bread share many of the same basic ingredients,
and America has enjoyed parallel renaissances in the brewing of beer and
the baking of bread. So it's possible once more to wash down a fresh,
crispy loaf with fresh, hoppy ale on this side of the Atlantic.
European bakers have long produced specialty
breads that depend on beer for their basic character; and porter
cake—rich with raisins, nuts, glacé cherries, and orange peel—
was an after-dinner favorite in Ireland that immigrants from
Sligo and Limerick brought to the New World.
More surprisingly, perhaps, fruit-flavored beers
can find their way into every kind of dessert
from trifles to sorbets.

CHOCOLATE FLOURLESS TORTE

8 SERVINGS

This is a chocolate lover's delight. Watch out for friends who eat more than their share or you'll never serve eight.

	Cocoa powder, for dusting the pan
11	ounces semisweet chocolate, *finely chopped*
1	cup plus 6 tablespoons unsalted butter
⅓	cups confectioners' sugar
7	eggs
⅓	cup Hops® Stout

Preheat the oven to 300°F. Butter a 9-inch springform pan and dust the bottom and sides with the cocoa, shaking out any excess. In a double boiler, melt the chocolate and butter over very low heat, stirring occasionally. Pour into a large bowl and cool to room temperature. Sift the confectioners' sugar into the chocolate mixture and stir to blend well. With an electric mixer, beat in the eggs one at a time, beating well after each addition. Add the stout and mix well. Pour the batter into the prepared pan and place it in a larger baking pan filled with about ½ inch of hot water. Bake for about 1 ½ hours, or until the center is firm to the touch. Chill in the refrigerator 6 hours or overnight. To serve, remove the sides of the pan.

If Hops® Stout is not available, use Anderson Valley® Stout or see Substitution Chart.

LIME BEER SOUFFLÉS

6 SERVINGS

CHEF
JONNA J. JENSEN

I CUGINI
SANTA MONICA, CA

*Beer and lime add a mysterious touch of bitterness
to a sweet dessert soufflé.*

¾	cup milk
	Zest of 1 lime, *minced*
4	egg yolks
½	cup plus 1 tablespoon sugar
6	tablespoons all-purpose flour
¾	cup Rhino Chasers® American Amber Ale
6	egg whites
	Pinch of salt
	Confectioners' sugar, for dusting

Preheat the oven to 400°F. Generously butter six (6-ounce) soufflé cups and sprinkle them with sugar, tapping out the excess.

Combine the milk and zest in a medium saucepan. Scald and remove from the heat. Cover and let steep 10 to 15 minutes.

In a medium bowl, whisk the egg yolks with ½ cup of the sugar until pale and fluffy. Add the flour and mix well. Gradually pour in the warm milk and the ale, stirring constantly, and then pour the mixture back into the saucepan. Simmer over medium heat, stirring constantly, for about 2 minutes, or until thick and smooth. Transfer to a bowl, cover with plastic, and set aside.

In a clean, dry bowl, whisk the egg whites and salt with an electric mixer until frothy. Sprinkle in the remaining tablespoon of sugar and beat until stiff and glossy. Spoon one third of the egg whites into the yolk mixture and gently fold in. Add the remaining whites and fold in just until the whites disappear.

Spoon into the prepared cups and place on a baking sheet. Bake 10 minutes, reduce the heat to 375°F., and bake 10 minutes longer. Remove from the oven, dust with confectioners' sugar, and serve immediately.

If Rhino Chasers® American Amber Ale is not available, see Substitution Chart.

CHOCOLATE, STOUT, AND BANANA SOUP WITH INDIVIDUAL ORANGE MARMALADE SOUFFLÉS

8 SERVINGS

The chocolate and banana combination has long been recognized as bliss-inducing, but stout adds a whole new dimension to the equation.

8	ounces high-quality semi-sweet chocolate, *finely chopped*
1 ½	cups sugar
3	tablespoons unsalted butter, *softened*
¼	teaspoon salt
2	cups heavy cream
1	cup Anderson Valley® Stout
1 ½	cups pureed ripe bananas
1	teaspoon vanilla extract

Melt the chocolate in the top of a double boiler over simmering water, stirring frequently. When the chocolate is melted, stir in the sugar, butter, and salt.

Slowly stir in the cream and stout. Remove the top pan, and place directly on a burner over low heat, stirring to dissolve the sugar and to blend all the ingredients, for 3 to 5 minutes. Stir in the banana and vanilla. Set aside and keep warm.

INDIVIDUAL SOUFFLÉS

3	tablespoons all-purpose flour
3	tablespoons plus 2 teaspoons sugar
½	cup plus 2 tablespoons milk
4	egg yolks
1 ½	tablespoons unsalted butter
6	tablespoons English orange marmalade, *pureed*
5	egg whites
	Dash of salt
	Fresh mint sprigs, for garnish

Preheat the oven to 375°F. Butter and flour eight large nonstick muffin cups. In a medium saucepan over low heat, stir together the flour and 3 tablespoons of the sugar. Gradually add the milk, stirring until well blended. Raise the heat to medium and cook, stirring constantly, until the mixture starts to thicken and boil. Remove from the heat and cool to room temperature, stirring constantly. Add the egg yolks, one at a time, beating well after each addition. Beat in the butter and marmalade and set aside.

In a medium bowl with an electric mixer, beat the egg whites with the salt until peaks start to form. Sprinkle in the remaining 2 teaspoons of sugar and beat until soft peaks form. Stir one third of the egg whites into the egg yolk mixture, then gently fold in the remaining egg whites. Pour the mixture into the prepared cups. Place in lower third of the oven and immediately reduce the temperature to 350°F. Bake for 10 to 12 minutes or until the tops are golden but the centers are slightly moist.

To serve, ladle the soup into eight shallow-rimmed bowls. Run a knife around each soufflé to gently unmold and place a soufflé in the center of each bowl. Garnish with the mint.

If Anderson Valley® Stout is not available, see Substitution Chart.

Note:
Additional
presentation ideas:
1/ Pipe whipped cream
on the soup at the
base of the
individual soufflés.
As the cream melts
from the heat of
the soup, make a
design by dragging
the tip of a knife
through the cream
and the soup.
2/ Before ladling
the soup into the
bowls, dust the rims
with confectioners'
sugar and sprinkle
with a few
edible flowers.

RHINO CHASERS ALE CAKE

12 TO 16 SERVINGS

A light and flavorful combination of fruits, nuts, and ale. Serve with whipped cream or vanilla ice cream, if desired.

1 1/4	cups sifted all-purpose flour
1 1/2	teaspoons ground allspice
	Dash each of ground nutmeg and ground cloves
1	cup unsalted butter, *softened*
1	cup packed light brown sugar
4	eggs
	Zest of one medium orange
	Zest of one medium lemon
3/4	cup dried cranberries
3/4	cup raisins
3/4	cup golden raisins
1/2	cup chopped pecans
3/4	cup Rhino Chasers® American Amber Ale

Preheat the oven to 325°F. Grease and lightly flour a 9-inch-round springform pan. Sift together the flour, allspice, nutmeg, and cloves. In a large mixing bowl, beat together the butter and brown sugar until smooth. Beat in eggs one at a time. Add the flour mixture and beat until blended. Stir in the orange and lemon zest, the cranberries, raisins, pecans, and ¼ cup of the ale. Pour into the prepared pan and bake 1 hour. Reduce the heat to 300°F. and continue baking 1 hour longer. (The cake will collapse slightly in the center.) Cool in the pan on a wire rack for 30 minutes. Remove from the pan and cool completely. With a thin wooden or metal skewer, pierce holes 1 inch apart all over the top of the cake. Spoon the remaining ½ cup of ale over the cake. Cover it tightly with plastic wrap and then in aluminum foil, and refrigerate at least 1 week before serving. The cake may be refrigerated for several months.

If Rhino Chasers® American Amber Ale is not available, see Substitution Chart.

GINGERBREAD

I LOAF

Serve this groundbreaking ale-tinged ginger cake with the traditional toppings—whipped crème fraîche or vanilla ice cream—for a holiday treat.

1 ⅓	cups flour
1	tablespoon baking soda
1 ¼	tablespoons ground ginger
1	tablespoon allspice
1	stick unsalted butter, *melted*
½	cup molasses
⅔	cup sugar
2	eggs, beaten
¾	cup Rhino Chasers® American Amber Ale

Preheat the oven to 350°F. Grease and flour a 9 x 5 x 3-inch loaf pan. Sift together the flour, baking soda, ginger, and allspice into a mixing bowl.

In another bowl, whisk together the butter, molasses, sugar, and eggs. Make a well in the center of the flour mixture and pour in the beer and egg mixture. Stir until smooth and pour into the prepared pan. Bake for 30 to 35 minutes, until the center springs back when pressed. Cool on a rack, still in the pan, and serve warm or at room temperature.

If Rhino Chasers® American Amber Ale is not available, see Substitution Chart.

NORMAN STEWART

FOOD STYLIST
LOS ANGELES, CA

RAISIN, SPICE, AND HAZELNUT BREAD PUDDING

8 SERVINGS

This homey pudding is best served warm from the oven, with whipped cream or a scoop of vanilla ice cream.

9	slices cinnamon-raisin bread, *cut into cubes* (about 6 cups)
½	cup hazelnuts
1	cup Rhino Chasers® American Amber Ale
1	cup heavy cream
1	cup milk
4	eggs
½	cup packed light brown sugar
2	tablespoons butter, *melted and cooled slightly*
½	teaspoon pumpkin pie spice
¼	teaspoon salt
	Freshly grated zest of 1 medium orange

Preheat the oven to 350°F. Butter a 2-quart soufflé dish or casserole. Arrange the bread cubes in a single layer on one side of a large baking sheet. Place the nuts on the other side. Bake for 10 minutes to lightly toast the bread and the nuts. Remove from the oven and cool slightly.

In a large bowl, combine the ale, cream, and milk. Add the bread cubes and mix to coat evenly. Soak 30 minutes, stirring occasionally. Meanwhile, coarsely chop the nuts and set aside.

In a medium bowl, lightly whisk the eggs. Add the brown sugar, melted butter, pumpkin pie spice, and salt. Lightly beat to dissolve the sugar. Add the egg mixture to the bread and stir to combine. Stir in the orange zest and the chopped nuts. Pour into prepared dish. Place the dish in a baking pan filled with about ½ inch of hot water and bake for 1 ¼ hours, until the pudding is puffy and firm to the touch. Remove from the water bath and cool 10 minutes. Serve warm.

If Rhino Chasers® American Amber Ale is not available, see Substitution Chart.

SWEET CARROT AND BEER SORBET

4 TO 6 SERVINGS

You'll never believe how good this tastes until you freeze up a batch.

¼	cup sugar
2	tablespoons honey
¾	pound carrots, *thinly sliced*
1	cup Watney's® Cream Stout
2	tablespoons freshly squeezed orange juice
	Fresh mint sprigs, for garnish (optional)

In a small saucepan, combine ¾ cup water, the sugar, and honey. Bring to a boil, add the carrots and cook, covered, over medium-low heat for 15 to 20 minutes or until the carrots are very tender. Transfer the mixture to a food processor or blender along with the stout and orange juice. Blend until smooth. Pour into an 8 x 8-inch-square baking pan and freeze until firm. To serve, scoop into chilled goblets and garnish each serving with fresh mint sprigs, if desired.

If Watney's® Cream Stout is not available, see Substitution Chart.

CHEF
SHIGEFUMI TACHIBE

CHAYA BRASSERIE
LOS ANGELES, CA
CHAYA VENICE
VENICE, CA

GINGERED APRICOT ALE SORBET

4 TO 6 SERVINGS

*The effervescence of the ale in this refreshing summer sorbet
gives it an especially light texture.*

½	pound ripe apricots, *halved and pitted*
½	cup sugar
2	teaspoons grated fresh ginger
¾	cup Thomas Kemper® Apricot Ale, *chilled*

In a medium saucepan combine the apricots, 1 ½ cups water, sugar, and ginger. Bring to a boil, stirring occasionally. Reduce the heat and simmer, covered, until the apricots are very tender, about 10 minutes. Cool and puree in a food processor or blender until smooth. Chill the puree and stir in the chilled ale. Freeze in an ice cream freezer, following the manufacturer's directions.

If Thomas Kemper® Apricot Ale is not available, see Substitution Chart.

ROOT BEER FLAN

A creamy, yet light flan with a delicious flavor.

1 ¼	cups sugar
⅓	cup St. Stan's® Red Alt
3	whole eggs
3	egg yolks
1	cup milk
¾	cup flat root beer
2	tablespoons heavy cream
2	tablespoons coarsely chopped fresh ginger
1	bag sarsaparilla tea
1	stick Mexican cinnamon
1	teaspoon barley malt syrup *(see Headnote, page 134)*
	Fresh mint leaves, for garnish

Place 1 cup of the sugar in a small heavy saucepan over medium heat. Add the ale and swirl to dissolve the sugar (do not stir). Bring to a boil without stirring, reduce the heat, and simmer until the mixture turns dark amber in color. Remove from the heat and immediately pour into six (4-ounce) custard cups, swirling to coat the sides and bottoms.

Preheat the oven to 350°F. To prepare the custard mixture: In a large bowl, beat together the whole eggs and egg yolks and set aside. In a medium saucepan, combine all the remaining ingredients except the garnish. Bring to a steady simmer and reduce by about one half, about 5 minutes. Remove and discard the teabag and the cinnamon stick. Gradually whisk a small amount of the hot milk mixture into the eggs. Whisking constantly, gradually add all the milk mixture. Strain the custard through a fine sieve and pour it into the caramel-coated custard cups. Place the cups in a baking pan filled with about ¾ inch of hot water. Carefully place the pan in the oven and lay a sheet of aluminum foil over the cups.

Bake for 30 minutes or until the custard is set. Remove from the water bath and cool completely. To serve, run a small knife around the inside of the cups and carefully invert the custards into individual dessert plates. Garnish with the mint leaves.

If St. Stan's® Red Alt is not available, see Substitution Chart.

CHEF
STEPHEN CARRASCO

SUNSET MARQUIS
HOTEL AND VILLAS
WEST HOLLYWOOD, CA

DEEP–FRIED APPLE FRITTERS WITH CARAMEL SAUCE

6 TO 8 SERVINGS

The ingredients are simple, but this is definitely a special-occasion dessert. The caramel sauce can be made in advance and gently reheated before serving.

⅓	cup milk at room temperature
1	teaspoon active dry yeast
1	cup flour
½	teaspoon salt
⅓	cup Rhino Chasers® Lager beer
1	egg yolk
2	quarts plus 2 teaspoons vegetable oil
4 to 5	Granny Smith apples
	Freshly squeezed lemon juice
2	egg whites
¼	cup granulated sugar
	Confectioners' sugar, for dusting
	Warm Caramel Sauce (see page 181)
	Fresh mint leaves, for garnish

In a small bowl, stir together half the milk and the yeast. Set aside. In a large bowl, stir together the flour and salt. Add the remaining milk, the beer, egg yolk, and 2 teaspoons of the oil. Add until the batter is smooth. Beat in the milk-yeast mixture and beat well. Cover with plastic wrap and set aside at room temperature for 1 ½ to 2 hours.

Peel, core, and slice the apples into ½-inch-thick rings. Sprinkle the apple slices with the lemon juice to prevent them from browning.

In a deep-fryer, heat the 2 quarts of oil to 375°F. Just before frying, beat the egg whites until foamy with an electric mixer. Gradually add the granulated sugar and beat until soft peaks form. Gently fold the egg whites into the batter. Dip a few of the apple slices into the batter, then carefully slip them into the heated oil. Cook until one side is lightly browned, then turn with a fork to brown the second side, about 5 minutes altogether. Remove and drain on paper towels. Dust with confectioners' sugar and keep warm while preparing the remaining fritters. To serve, spoon 2 to 3 tablespoons warm caramel sauce onto individual dessert plates and arrange three or four of the apple fritters over the sauce. Garnish with fresh mint leaves.

WARM CARAMEL SAUCE – Makes about 1 ¼ cups

| ½ | cup sugar |
| 1 | cup heavy cream |

In a medium saucepan, combine the sugar and 1 ⅓ cup water and cook over medium heat, stirring, just until the sugar dissolves. Continue cooking at a brisk simmer without stirring, until the mixture turns amber in color, about 15 minutes. Remove from the heat and gradually whisk in the heavy cream.

If Rhino Chasers® Lager beer is not available, see Substitution Chart.

BEER CREPES WITH SAUTÉED PEARS

8 SERVINGS

A hint of beer adds dimension to these delicate paper-thin crepes.

CREPES

2	eggs
1	tablespoon sugar
⅔	cup flour
2	tablespoons butter, *melted*
½	cup milk
½	cup Rhino Chasers® American Amber Ale

In a medium mixing bowl, whisk together the eggs, sugar, and flour until smooth. Pour in 1 tablespoon of the butter, the milk, and the ale, whisking continuously to combine. Cover and set aside 30 minutes at room temperature.

To cook, lightly brush a 9-inch, nonstick skillet with some of the remaining melted butter and warm over medium heat. Pour in ¼ cup of the batter and swirl the pan to coat it evenly. When the edges of the crepe are golden, flip and cook it 20 seconds on the other side. Stack the crepes on a plate, separated by wax paper, between crepes, until all the batter is used. Cover with towel and set aside.

PEARS

5	firm medium pears, *peeled and cored*
6	tablespoons granulated sugar
3	tablespoons fresh lemon juice
3	tablespoons unsalted butter
	Confectioners' sugar, for dusting

Cut the pears into ½-inch cubes and transfer them to a mixing bowl. Toss with the sugar and lemon juice.

Melt the butter in a medium skillet over medium heat. Add the pear mixture and cook until tender but still firm, about 5 minutes. Spread the crepes on a counter. Spoon equal amounts of filling onto each crepe. Gently roll up and transfer the crepes to serving plates. Sprinkle with confectioners' sugar and serve.

If Rhino Chasers® American Amber Ale is not available, see Substitution Chart.

CHEDDAR CHEESECAKE WITH
SPICED PEAR TOPPING

PEGGY MELLODY

FOOD CONSULTANT,

WRITER,

EDITOR,

AND

COOKING INSTRUCTOR

LOS ANGELES, CA

12 SERVINGS

This is too wonderful a cheesecake to enjoy only in the fall and winter months. In the summer, substitute summer red or yellow Bartlett pears.

CRUST

1	cup all-purpose flour
¼	cup sugar
½	teaspoon freshly grated lemon zest
½	cup unsalted butter, *chilled and cut into 1-inch pieces*
2	egg yolks, *lightly beaten*
½	teaspoon vanilla extract

Preheat the oven to 400°F. In a medium bowl, combine the flour, sugar, and lemon zest. With a pastry blender or two knives, cut in the butter until the mixture resembles coarse crumbs. Add the egg yolks and vanilla, mixing well. Press the mixture onto the bottom and up the sides of a 9- or 10-inch springform pan. Bake for 5 minutes. Remove from the oven and set aside until ready to fill. Reduce the oven temperature to 325°F.

FILLING

4	(8-ounce) packages cream cheese, *softened*
1 ½	cups freshly grated Cheddar cheese
1 ½	cups sugar
3	tablespoons cornstarch
6	eggs
¼	cup sour cream
¼	cup Rhino Chasers® Lager beer

In a large mixing bowl with an electric mixer at medium speed, beat together the cheeses until smooth. Add the sugar and cornstarch and beat until well blended. Add the eggs, one at a time, blending well after each addition. Add the sour cream and beer and beat just until blended. Pour the filling mixture into the baked crust. Bake 1 hour, then turn the oven off with the door slightly ajar, and cool the cheesecake completely.

SPICED PEAR TOPPING AND GARNISH

4 to 6	Bosc or Anjou pears, *peeled, cored, and sliced* (about 3 cups)
½	cup unsweetened apple juice
¼	cup sugar
½	teaspoon vanilla extract
I	tablespoon cornstarch
¼	teaspoon ground cinnamon
	Freshly grated lemon and orange zest, for garnish

In a large saucepan, combine the sliced pears and ¼ cup of the apple juice. Bring to a boil, reduce the heat, and simmer, covered, until the pears are crisp-tender, about 5 minutes. Do not overcook. Remove from the heat and add the sugar, stirring until the sugar dissolves. Gradually stir in the remaining ¼ cup of apple juice and the vanilla. In a cup, stir together the cornstarch and cinnamon. Add the cornstarch mixture to the pears and cook over medium heat until the sauce is thickened and clear, stirring occasionally, about 2 minutes. Remove from the heat and cool completely, stirring occasionally.

Arrange the pear slices on top of the cooled cheesecake and spoon the remaining sauce over them. Cover and refrigerate 6 hours or overnight. To serve, remove the sides from the springform pan and sprinkle the cake with the grated lemon and orange zest.

If Rhino Chasers® Lager beer is not available, see Substitution Chart.

Copyright Taylor Publishing, Dallas, Texas (Sweet Celebrations, 1991)

BLACKHOOK BISCOTTI WITH GARAM MASALA ROASTED CASHEWS

MAKES 5 DOZEN

These are delicious as an appetizer or as part of a cheese course along with a blue cheese like Stilton or Gorganzola. Add some fresh fruit such as cherries and plums.

4	cups all-purpose flour
¼	cup sugar
1	teaspoon baking powder
½	teaspoon salt
5	eggs
½	cup Blackhook® Porter
¼	cup vegetable oil
2	cups Garam Masala Roasted Cashews (see below)

Preheat the oven to 350°F. Line a large baking sheet with parchment paper. In a large mixing bowl, whisk together the flour, sugar, baking powder, and salt. With the paddle attachment of an electric mixer, beat 4 of the eggs, the porter, and oil with the flour mixture for 1 to 2 minutes until blended. Add the cashews and mix 1 minute longer. The mixture will look somewhat "shaggy." (If a paddle attachment is not available, first beat in the eggs, porter, and oil, then stir in the cashews.)

Turn the mixture out onto a lightly floured surface and divide it into three equal portions. Roll each one into a 12-inch log. Place the logs on the prepared baking sheet.

With a whisk, beat the remaining egg with 2 tablespoons of water. Lightly brush the tops of the logs with the egg mixture. Bake for 20 minutes, then remove from the oven and cool slightly. Reduce the oven temperature to 300°F. Slice the rolls diagonally into ¼- to ½-inch slices. Arrange the slices, cut sides up, on baking sheets, and bake for 10 minutes per side, or until crisp and light golden in color. Cool completely. They will keep in an airtight container for about 2 weeks.

GARAM MASALA ROASTED CASHEWS - Makes 2 cups

2	cups raw cashews
2	tablespoons unsalted butter

| 2 | tablespoons garam masala *(see page 200)* |
| ½ | teaspoon salt |

Preheat the oven to 350°F. In a medium bowl, combine the cashews, butter, garam masala, and salt, mixing well to coat the nuts. Arrange in a single layer in a baking pan and bake for 8 to 10 minutes, or until the nuts are lightly toasted.

If Blackhook® Porter is not available, see Substitution Chart.

PYRAMID HEFEWEIZEN
BREAD STICKS

MAKES 24

Because they have several risings, bake these in advance.
Serve them with a zesty wheat beer.

1	(¼-ounce) package active dry yeast
½	teaspoon sugar
1	cup warm water (105° to 115°F.)
¼	cup Pyramid® Hefeweizen Ale
1	tablespoon Worcestershire sauce
1	tablespoon olive oil
3 ½	cups unbleached all-purpose flour
1	tablespoon fresh thyme, *crushed*
1 to 2	teaspoons coarsely ground black pepper
1	teaspoon salt
½	cup finely grated Gruyère cheese
	Sesame or poppy seeds

In a large bowl, stir the yeast and sugar into the warm water. Let stand a few minutes. Stir in the ale, Worcestershire sauce, and olive oil. In another bowl, stir together the flour, thyme, pepper, and salt. Add to the yeast mixture and combine. Turn the dough out onto a lightly floured surface and knead until smooth and slightly sticky, about 5 minutes. Transfer the dough to a greased bowl, turning to coat all sides. Cover and let rise in a warm place until doubled in bulk, about 1 hour.

Remove and punch down the dough. Place it on a lightly floured surface and sprinkle with the cheese. Knead in the cheese for about 5 minutes. Return the dough to the greased bowl; cover, and let rise again until doubled.

Punch down again and turn out onto a lightly floured surface. Divide the dough in half. Roll each half into a 12-inch-long rectangle. Cut crosswise into twelve pieces. Roll each piece on a floured surface with the palms of your hands to form a rope about ⅓ inch thick. Roll the ropes in the seeds and place them on greased cookie sheets. Cover and let rise until doubled, 45 to 60 minutes.

To bake, preheat the oven to 400°F. Lightly brush the ropes with heavily salted water and bake 15 to 20 minutes, until brown and crispy. Remove from the baking sheet and cool on racks.

If Pyramid® Hefeweizen Ale is not available, see Substitution Chart.

HERBFARM WALNUT ALE BREAD

3 LOAVES

Placing the dough to rise in wicker baskets gives
the baked bread a distinct pattern.

CHEF
JERRY TRAUNFELD

THE HERBFARM
FALL CITY, WA

2 ½	cups Full Sail® Amber Ale
1	tablespoon active dry yeast
¼	cup honey
5 ½ to 6	cups bread flour
1 ½	cups chopped walnuts, *toasted*
1	tablespoon chopped fresh rosemary
1	tablespoon salt
	Cornmeal, for dusting

Bring the ale to a boil in a medium saucepan. Pour it into a large bowl and cool to
lukewarm, about 105°F. Sprinkle the yeast over the ale and let it stand a few minutes.
Add the honey and stir to dissolve. Add 3 cups of the flour and beat well. Cover with plastic
wrap and let stand overnight at room temperature.

Stir in all the remaining ingredients except the cornmeal, adding enough of the
flour to make a medium to soft dough. Turn the dough onto a lightly floured surface and
knead until smooth, about 10 minutes. Place the dough in a greased bowl, turning to coat
it on all sides. Cover and let rise in a warm place (80° to 85°F.) until doubled in bulk, about
1 hour. Punch down the dough and divide it into three pieces. On a lightly floured surface,
roll each piece into a tight ball and place the balls, smooth side down, into 8- to 10-inch-
round, lightly floured wicker baskets. Cover and let rise in a warm place until doubled,
about 45 to 60 minutes.

Place a large pizza stone or unglazed quarry tiles on the oven rack. Preheat the
oven to 400°F.

Sprinkle the stone with cornmeal. When bread has doubled in size, turn the loaves
out of the baskets upside down, onto the stone. With a sharp knife, slash three slits on the
top of each loaf. Bake 40 to 45 minutes or until brown and crusty.

If Full Sail® Amber Ale is not available, see Substitution Chart.

BERNARD CLAYTON, JR.

COOKBOOK AUTHOR
BLOOMINGTON, IN

BUTTER—BEER BATTER BREAD

I LOAF

For this aromatic loaf, a melted stick of butter is poured over the batter, which, while baking, slowly seeps to the bottom. Then the mixture is turned upside down so the butter goes back through the loaf, which becomes permeated with butter. This recipe comes from Georgia, where self-rising flour is widely used, as it is in most of the South.

3	cups self-rising flour *(see Note)*
¼	cup sugar
½	teaspoon salt
I	(12-ounce) bottle Rhino Chasers® Lager beer
½	cup finely chopped fresh oregano leaves
½	cup unsalted butter, melted

Preheat the oven to 350°F. Grease an 8 ½ x 4 ½-inch loaf pan. By hand or with an electric mixer: Combine the flour, sugar, and salt in a mixing bowl. Add the beer and oregano leaves. With a wooden spoon or the paddle attachment of the electric mixer, beat the batter for a few minutes to blend thoroughly.

If using a food processor: Attach the steel blade. Place the flour, sugar, and salt in the work bowl. Pulse twice to mix the dry ingredients. With the machine running, pour in the beer and add the chopped oregano. Stop the machine when the ingredients are just blended.

Pour or spoon the batter into the prepared pan. Pour the warm butter carefully over the top of the batter. It will not be absorbed until the baking begins. Bake the loaf for 45 or 50 minutes, or until golden brown. A toothpick or metal skewer inserted into the loaf should come out clean. (If using a convection oven, reduce the heat 50°F.)

Remove the pan from the oven and allow the loaf to cool for 15 minutes before removing it from the pan to a metal rack. Hold a baking rack against the top of the loaf and quickly but carefully turn it upside down so the top of the loaf is on the bottom. Set it aside to cool—and to allow the butter to drift back into the loaf.

If Rhino Chasers® Lager beer is not available, see Substitution Chart.

Note:
If self-rising flour is not at hand, substitute an equal amount of all-purpose flour plus 1 tablespoon baking powder and an additional ½ teaspoon salt.

DARK SOUR BREAD

2 LOAVES

There are four different wheat products plus cornmeal plus beer in this almost-black loaf of delicious bread. The bread, which has a moist, chewy texture, is ideal for a buffet or just with a piece of sharp cheese as a snack.

2	cups flat beer
⅔	cup cornmeal
½	cup molasses
2	tablespoons unsalted butter
2	teaspoons salt
2	(¼-ounce) packages active dry yeast
½	cup each wheat germ and whole wheat bran cereal
1 ½	cups whole wheat flour
1	cup (approximately) bread flour or all-purpose flour

Bring the beer to a simmer in a large, heavy saucepan. Add the ½ cup water, remove from the heat, and stir in the cornmeal, molasses, butter, and salt. Let cool. When the mixture has cooled to lukewarm, stir in the yeast to dissolve.

Add the wheat germ, bran cereal, and whole wheat flour. Mix together with a wooden spoon. Slowly add the white flour, working it in with your fingers or a pastry blade. Continue to knead and work the dough by hand, adding white flour if necessary to control the stickiness, for about 8 to 10 minutes.

Place the dough into a large buttered bowl, cover it with plastic wrap, and let it rise at room temperature until doubled, about 2 hours. (If prepared with fast-rising yeast, reduce the rising times by half.) Divide the dough and shape the loaves into two long baguettes (ideal for small sandwiches), or round loaves. Transfer the loaves to a baking sheet. Cover with wax paper and let rise until doubled, about 1 ½ hours.

Preheat the oven to 350°F. 20 minutes before baking. Bake the loaves in the middle of the oven for 40 minutes, or until they are crusty and almost black. Midway, turn the sheet to bake evenly. (If using a convection oven, reduce the heat by 50°F.) Transfer the loaves to a metal rack to cool.

BERNARD CLAYTON, JR.

COOKBOOK AUTHOR
BLOOMINGTON, IN

*Note:
The loaves can be sliced thin, and make excellent toast. The bread will keep, wrapped in foil, for 2 weeks. This recipe is not recommended to be made with an electric mixer or in a food processor because the dough is too heavy.*

BERNARD CLAYTON, JR.

❧

COOKBOOK AUTHOR
BLOOMINGTON, IN

TWISTED CHEESE LOAF

2 LOAVES

Cheese and beer have always been the best of companions, but never more so than in this bread—a lovely braided yellow loaf—mellow with cheese and piquant with beer. This bread can be made one of three ways: by hand, mixer, or processor.

1	(12-ounce) bottle Sierra Nevada® Pale Ale
2	tablespoons unsalted butter
2	tablespoons sugar
1	tablespoon salt
1	(8-ounce) package processed Swiss or American cheese, *diced*
5	cups (approximately) bread flour or all-purpose flour
2	(¼-ounce) packages active dry yeast
8	ounces natural Swiss cheese, *cut into ¼-inch cubes*

Grease two 8 x 4-inch loaf pans.

In a large saucepan, combine the beer, the ½ cup water, the butter, sugar, salt, and processed cheese and heat until hot. The cheese need not melt completely. Remove from the heat and cool to lukewarm. Put 2 cups of the flour and the yeast in a large mixing bowl. Pour in the warm cheese mixture and beat by hand with a wooden spoon 100 strong strokes, or for 3 minutes at medium speed with the paddle attachment of an electric mixer. Stir in the remaining flour, ½ cup at a time, first with the spoon and then by hand. If using the mixer, change to a dough hook when the dough becomes too heavy to stir with the paddle. The dough will be a rough mass that will clean the sides of the bowl. If the dough continues to be slack and moisture breaks through, add small amounts of additional flour.

By hand: Turn the dough onto a lightly floured work surface and spread the Swiss cheese cubes over it. Fold the dough over on the cheese and knead with the rhythmic motion of push-turn-fold. The dough will become smooth and elastic, and bubbles will form under the surface. Break the kneading rhythm occasionally by throwing the dough down hard against the work surface.

By mixer: Drop the cheese bits into the bowl while the mixer is running. The dough will clean the sides of the bowl and form a ball around the revolving hook. If it does not, sprinkle it with additional flour. Knead by hand or mixer for 10 minutes.

By processor: Combine all the ingredients except the flour, yeast, and Swiss cheese in a large saucepan, as above. Attach the plastic dough blade. Measure 3 ½ cups flour and the yeast into the processor work bowl. Pulse to blend. With the motor running, slowly pour a portion of the cooled cheese mixture through the feed tube to form a wet mass in the bowl. Do not make it a thin batter. Keep it on the heavy side. Take off the cover and add ¾ cup flour. Pulse several times until the flour is completely absorbed. With the processor running, add the balance of the cheese mixture and flour, ¼ cup at a time, until the dough forms a ball and is carried around the bowl by the force of the blade. With the machine running, knead for 50 seconds. When first turned out of the work bowl, the dough will be slightly sticky, but a dusting of flour will take the stickiness away. Work the cheese bits into the dough by hand.

For the first rising, place the dough in a large buttered bowl and turn it over to coat completely and prevent crusting. Cover the bowl with plastic wrap and leave at room temperature until the dough has doubled in volume, about 1 hour. (If prepared with fast-rising yeast and at the recommended higher temperatures, reduce the rising times by half.)

Punch down and knead the dough for 30 seconds. Divide the dough in half. (Each half will weigh about 1 ½ pounds.) Roll each half into a 12 x 6-inch rectangle. Cut each rectangle lengthwise into three 2-inch strips leaving them joined at one end by a ½-inch piece. Braid the strips. Tuck under the ends to make the dough about the same length as the baking pans. Place it in the prepared pans, place the pans in a warm place, cover with wax or parchment paper, and leave until the center of the dough has risen ½-inch above the edge of the pan, about 45 minutes.

Preheat the oven to 350°F. 20 minutes before baking.

Bake until the loaves are golden brown, about 45 minutes. They are done when tapping the bottom crust yields a hard, hollow sound. If not, return the loaves to the oven for 5 to 10 minutes longer. Midway during baking, and again near the end, shift the loaves so they are exposed equally to the temperature variations in the oven. If the loaves appear to be browning too quickly, cover them with aluminum foil. (If using a convection oven, reduce the heat by 50°F.)

Remove the bread from the oven, turn it out of the pans, and place the loaves on a metal rack to cool before slicing.

If Sierra Nevada® Pale Ale is not available, see Substitution Chart.

THE CHEFS AND PERSONALITIES

BRUCE AIDELLS
AIDELL'S SAUSAGE COMPANY
1625 ALVARADO STREET
SAN LEANDRO, CA 94577
510 614 5450

Bruce Aidells was working as an endocrinologist in London when he made his first sausage, after which his life began to change. While doing postdoctoral research at Berkeley, he began to sell his homemade sausages and pâtés to Bay Area restaurants and eventually exchanged his lab coat for an apron and toque. In 1983 he founded Aidells Sausage Company and soon his unique hand-crafted charcuterie was a staple on the menus of top restaurants in many parts of the country. He is the author or co-author of six books, including *Hot Links and Country Flavors* and *Real Beer and Good Eats.*

DEBBIE ALLEN

Award-winning actress, dancer, choreographer, and director, Debbie Allen is also an accomplished cook, whose friends appreciate such specialties as her Honey-Roasted Lamb. After success on Broadway and her first Tony nomination for *West Side Story,* Debbie charmed the television audiences as the dance teacher in *Fame,* for which she received two Emmys and a Golden Globe award. She was director-producer of *A Different World,* has choreographed the Academy Awards for five consecutive years, and has received the prestigious Essence Award.

JEFFREY JOSEPH ANDERSON
GORDON BIERSCH BREWERY RESTAURANT
41 HUGUS ALLEY
PASADENA, CA 91103
818 449 0052

Jeffrey Joseph Anderson is executive chef of the Gordon Biersch Brewery restaurants, a position that entails overseeing kitchen operations in five locations—Palo Alto, San Jose, San Francisco, Pasadena, and Honolulu. His mission is to ensure that each establishment reflects the uniqueness of its locality while adhering to the Biersch international-style American brewery cuisine,

which features an array of American Southwestern, Mediterranean, and Asian elements.

TIM ANDERSON
CAFE MARIMBA
1100 BURLINGAME AVENUE
BURLINGAME, CA 94010
415 347 0111

Tim Anderson's first restaurant, Routh Street Café, opened in Dallas in 1983 and almost immediately gained recognition as one of the best in the country. Over the next ten years he and partner Stephan Pyles opened three more—Baby Routh, Tejas, and Goodfellows—and Anderson was chosen by *Food & Wine* as one of the ten best new chefs in America. He is currently executive chef at Reed Hearon's Cafe Marimba in Burlingame, California.

FRANCESCO ANTONUCCI
REMI
145 WEST 53RD STREET
NEW YORK, NY 10019
212 581 4242

Venetian-born Francesco Antonucci, chef and co-owner of the bicoastal Remi restaurants, began his American career at the acclaimed Valentino restaurant in Santa Monica, California. He then joined forces with film producer Dino de Laurentis at the DDL Foodshow and the DDL Bistro in Manhattan's Trump Tower before opening the New York edition of Remi, which was selected Best Italian Restaurant in America by the Luigi Veronelli guidebook. Mr. Antonucci has also authored two Italian cookbooks: *Il Sapore Della Memoria (The Flavor of the Memory)* and *Venetian Taste.*

LYNNE ARONSON
LOLA
30 WEST 22ND STREET
NEW YORK, NY 10010
212 675 6700

Executive chef of New York's Lola restaurant, Lynne Aronson began her career as a painter, a career that is reflected in the vivid colors and complex textures of her food. After attending the New York Restaurant School, she honed her skills at the Union Square Café and John Clancy's East. Considered by *Esquire* to be one of America's top ten young chefs, Aronson is credited with transforming Lola's from an island-themed hot spot into a restaurant respected for its authentically creative cuisine.

OCTAVIO RENÉ BECERRA
PINOT BISTRO
12969 VENTURA BOULEVARD
STUDIO CITY, CA 91604
818 990 0500

Octavio René Becerra planned a career in commercial photography, but exchanged his tripod for a toque under the inspiration of Chef Joachim Splichal, who is now Chef Becerra's partner in ventures such as Patina restaurant, on Los Angeles's fashionable Melrose strip, and Cafe Pinot in downtown L.A.

SCOTT BIRCH
BLACKHAWK LODGE
41 EAST SUPERIOR
CHICAGO, IL 60611
312 280 4080

Scott Birch is executive chef of Blackhawk Lodge, one of Chicago's most highly regarded eating spots. His wide experience includes stints with top flight kitchens in California and Hawaii. Like many of the best contemporary chefs, he places a strong emphasis on using fresh local produce.

CHRISTOPHER AND CATHERINE BROOKS

Beer critic Christopher Brooks acquired his initial expertise while living for six years in Belgium. He has visited hundreds of breweries worldwide, consulting with brewers and sampling thousands of beers. He has written about beer since 1984, becoming *Country Living* magazine's beer columnist in 1987. He has also contributed to the *New York Times*, *USA Today*, *Family Circle*, and the *Christian Science Monitor*. Both he and his wife, Catherine (photo not available) reside in Connecticut.

SCOTT BRYAN
LUMA RESTAURANT
200 9TH AVENUE
NEW YORK, NY 10011
212 633 8033

Scott Bryan began his cooking career in Boston, then moved to New York, where he gained experience at several top establishments, becoming executive chef at the romantically-stylish Alison on Dominick before moving to Luma Restaurant in Chelsea, where he is both executive chef and part owner.

SUSAN BUTTERFIELD
MATCH RESTAURANT
160 MERCER STREET
NEW YORK NY 10012
212 343 0020

A graduate of the Culinary Institute of America, Susan Butterfield presents her creative cuisine at New York's fashionable Match restaurant in SoHo, where she uses her background in Italian and French cooking to enhance a Pacific Rim menu. A great believer in the use of organic and regional ingredients, she also has had extensive catering experience.

STEPHEN CARRASCO
SUNSET MARQUIS HOTEL AND VILLAS
1200 NORTH ALTA LOMA ROAD
WEST HOLLYWOOD, CA 90069
310 657 1333

San Diego-born chef Carrasco began his culinary career as a food supervisor at the famous Hotel Coronado in San Diego, and rose to the position of executive chef in only six years. Carrasco is now in charge of the kitchen at the Sunset Marquis Hotel and Villas in Hollywood, where he features a "California Eclectic" cuisine that emphasizes freshness and originality, transforming ordinary ingredients into extraordinary dining experiences.

PIERRE CASSANOVA
CAFE DES ARTISTES
1534 NORTH MCCADDEN PLACE
LOS ANGELES, CA 90028
213 461 6889

Formerly the proprietor of Le Demi Lune, a highly regarded restaurant in Dole, France, Pierre Casanova is now the executive chef of Hollywood's Cafe Des Artistes, a meeting place for L.A.'s creative community that uses its profits to support the adjacent Stages theater, a long-established showcase for quality drama.

BERNARD CLAYTON, JR.

After a varied career as newspaperman, war correspondent, and book editor, Bernard Clayton, Jr., now devotes all his time to writing about food and travel. He is the author of four best-selling cookbooks, including *The Complete Book of Soups and Stews, The Complete Book of Pastry, The Breads of France,* and *Bernard Clayton's New Complete Book of Breads.* The last was a selection of the Literary Guild and winner of the R. T. French Tastemaker Award for outstanding specialty cookbook.

Eddie Garcia

ROBERT COCCA

SCHATZI ON MAIN
3110 MAIN STREET
SANTA MONICA, CA 90405
310 399 4800

Raised in New Jersey by Italian parents who loved to cook, and trained in part at Los Angeles's celebrated Spago restaurant, Robert Cocca now brings enthusiasm and flair to the menu of Arnold Schwarzenegger's Schatzi On Main, a favorite eaterie with L.A.'s show-business crowd. Chef Cocca's adventurous spirit is demonstrated by his recipe, included here, for Shrimp Sauté with Raspberry Lambic Sauce.

TERESA I. DELANEY

PYRAMID ALES/HART BREWING, INC.
110 WEST MARINE DRIVE
KALAMA, WA 98625
360 673 2121

Caterer and cook, Teresa I. Delaney is a passionate experimenter of new recipes, incorporating, whenever possible, the distinctive brews made by Pyramid Ales/Hart Brewing, Inc., with whom she has been associated for the past decade. An outstanding example of her achievement in this field is the Pyramid Hefeweizen Bread Sticks she contributed to this volume.

JOHN DICKINSON

WYNKOOP BREWING COMPANY
1634 18TH STREET
DENVER, CO 80202
303 297 2700

John Dickinson (no photo available) is one of several talented chefs and kitchen staff members of the Wynkoop Brewing Company, originator of Denver's landmark Wynkoop brewpub, an establishment that helped pioneer the notion that great beer should be matched with great food.

B. J. DOERFLING

The principal of B. J. Food Consulting, a Southern California company, B. J. Doerfling is a cookbook author and instructor of gourmet cooking as well as a globe-trotting connoisseur of fine food. Her expertise lies in the cuisines of Mexico, Spain, China, and Vietnam.

ROBERT DORNHELM

Robert Dornhelm is an Austrian born director of feature films, including *Fatal Deception, Requiem for Dominic, Echo Park,* and *She Dances Alone,* which won the Critics' Choice Award at the Cannes Film Festival. He has also produced and directed more than eighty documentaries, mostly for Austrian and German television.

CELESTINO DRAGO

DRAGO RISTORANTE
2628 WILSHIRE BOULEVARD
SANTA MONICA, CA 90403
310 828 1585

IL PISTAIO
141 SOUTH LAKE STREET
PASADENA, CA 91101
818 795 4006

400 NORTH CANNON
BEVERLY HILLS, CA 90210
310 205 5444

Celestino Drago grew up on a farm in northern Sicily where he and his family ate mozzarella made from the milk of their own cows, prosciutto from their pigs, and olive oil pressed from the fruit of their own trees. At the age of nineteen, he decided to make cooking his career. Serendipity brought him to Southern California, where he worked at Orlando Orsini and Chianti Cucina until opening his own restaurant—Celestino's Ristorante—in Beverly Hills in 1985. This venture was followed by the equally successful Drago in Santa Monica, as well as Il Pistaio in Beverly Hills and Pasadena.

PASCAL DROPSY
CORN MAIDEN COMPANY
10301 WASHINGTON BOULEVARD
CULVER CITY, CA 90232
310 202 6180

Pascal Dropsy has had wide experience in the world of food. In addition to being executive chef, executive sous chef, and pastry chef in several leading Belgian and American restaurants, including Le Dome in Los Angeles and Le Saint Jean des Prés in New York, he has served as private chef for a leading motion picture industry executive, cooking for such notables as President and Mrs. Bush. Currently, he is the owner of Corn Maiden Company, where gourmet tamales are handmade. These delicacies have led him to win two first prizes at The International Tamale Festival in Indio, California. Dropsy is also a food educator and organizer of the Hot and Spicy Food Festival in Pasadena, California.

WESLIE EVANS
THE GREAT LOST BEAR
540 FOREST AVENUE
PORTLAND, ME 04103
207 772 0300

Weslie Evans is chef and co-owner of The Great Lost Bear restaurant which has been a favorite with knowledgeable diners in Portland, Maine, since 1972. She is the originator of the Ginger Wheat Deep-Fried Fish Fillets that appears here.

CHRISTOPHER FINCH

With Scott Griffiths, Christopher Finch is the co-author of *America's Best Beers*. He is also the author of *Beer: A Connoisseur's Guide to the World's Best*, along with a score of other books, including such best-sellers as *The Art of Walt Disney* and *Rainbow: The Stormy Life of Judy Garland*. He is a frequent contributor to *Architectural Digest*.

MATT FLUKE
MARIN BREWING COMPANY
1809 LARKSPUR LANDING CIRCLE
LARKSPUR, CA 94939
415 461 4677

Matt Fluke holds the position of chef at the Calistoga Inn, Marin Brewing Company's popular brewpub located in the town of Larkspur, California, a ferry ride from San Francisco and a short hike from San Quentin Prison. Marin's excellent ales have won more medals at the Great American Beer Festival than those of any other brewery. Matt Fluke uses these brews in preparing hearty dishes that have helped make the Calistoga Inn a Bay Area institution.

MELISSA FLYNN
MERCHANT DU VIN CORPORATION
140 LAKESIDE AVENUE, SUITE 300
SEATTLE, WA 98122
206 322 5022

Melissa Flynn is a gifted self-taught chef whose career has been greatly influenced by her professional association with Charles Finkel, the proprietor of Seattle's Pike Place Brewery, one of America's top micros, and of Merchant du Vin Corporation, a company that imports some of Europe's finest beers. Catering for Merchant du Vin Corporation, and for events organized by Finkel, Ms. Flynn has become a notable expert in the art of cooking with high quality brews.

JANICE FRANKS
MENDOCINO BREWING COMPANY
13351 HIGHWAY 101 SOUTH
HOPLAND, CA 95449
707 744 1361

Janice Franks is a great believer in and advocate for the promotion of beer and food as a culinary experience, as is clear from her recipe for Grilled Red Tail Chicken Breast Salad with Salsa Vinaigrette. She has been associated with the Mendocino Brewing Company of Hopland, California—a pioneering craft beer producer—for ten years and served as the editor of the company's in-house cookbook *What Ales You?*

NICHOLAS M. GRAFF
HOPS! BISTRO & BREWERY
7000 EAST CAMELBACK ROAD
SCOTTSDALE, AZ 85251
602 945 4677

Current chef of Hops! Bistro & Brewery, Nicholas M. Graff is a graduate of the Culinary Institute of America and a specialist in Mexican and Southwestern cuisine. During his stint as executive chef at Epazote Regional Mexican Restaurant, he researched and developed recipes falling within the ethnic parameters established for the Epazote Baja Bar and Grill. He has also taught Mexican and Southwestern-style cooking.

MICKEY GRIFFITHS

Like so many great cooks, Mickey Griffiths (no photo available) ("mom") experiences the world's cuisine firsthand and possesses that gift of creating and recreating dishes by taste, not by recipe alone. Referring to herself as a "natural cook," Mickey taught for years at various women's groups and at the YMCA. Cooking for entertaining is her forté. When her husband was vice president at Chapman College, and Founder/Executive Director of Semester at Sea, she regularly prepared banquets for 30-100 people.

Art Montes de Oca

W. SCOTT GRIFFITHS

W. Scott Griffiths is the founder of William and Scott Brewing Company, the producers of Rhino Chasers® hand-crafted beer. The winner of many prestigious awards, Rhino Chasers is one of the fastest-growing craft beer in America today. Mr. Griffiths co-authored America's Best Beers: A Complete Guide to the More Than 350 Microbreweries and Brewpubs Across America and resides in Studio City, California.

E. K. Waller

LORETTA HWONG-GRIFFITHS

When she was very young, Loretta Hwong-Griffiths learned the techniques and nuances of Chinese cooking from her grandmother, T. C. Lu, an eminent Chinese opera star and master chef. Later she studied with the highly acclaimed teacher and cookbook author Madame T. S. Wong and has taken classes with such top chefs as Roy Yamaguchi, Vito Gnazzo, Ken Frank, and Jean Francois Meteigner. She is a member of Les Dames D'Escoffier.

BILLY HAHN
HARBORSIDE/MCCORMICK & SCHMICK
0309 S. W. MONTGOMERY
PORTLAND, OR 97201
503 220 1865

His love for the outdoors and search for a clean environment drew Chef Billy Hahn to Oregon in 1976. There he was introduced to the bounty of the Pacific Northwest. He worked at Horst Mager's Couch Street Fish House, then joined the McCormick & Schmick organization, for which he opened the Beaverton Fish House in 1981. In 1985 he opened the Harborside Restaurant to which a microbrewery was added in 1992.

SAM HAZEN
HEARTLAND BREWERY
35 UNION SQUARE WEST
NEW YORK, NY 10003
212 645 3400

A third-generation chef, Sam Hazen is executive chef of Manhattan's largest brewpub, the Heartland Brewery, in Union Square. After graduating from the Culinary Institute of America in 1982, Hazen worked at some of New York's most esteemed establishments—La Côte Basque, the Quilted Giraffe, and Quatorze, before moving on to London's three-star La Gavroche. At Heartland Brewery, his menu is a personal reinterpretation of pub favorites.

STEPHEN HINDY
BROOKLYN BREWERY
118 NORTH 11TH STREET
BROOKLYN, NY 11211
718 486 7422

With Tom Potter, Stephen Hindy is a founder of the Brooklyn Brewery and a partner in the Craft Brewer's Guild. As a correspondent and editor for *Newsweek* and the *Associated Press*, Hindy covered several foreign wars, which, he insists, provided an excellent schooling for starting a business in New York.

ROSEMARY HOWE
BARRAUD CATERERS LTD.
405 BROOME STREET
NEW YORK, NY 10013
212 925 1334

Based in New York's SoHo district, Rosemary Howe gives the lie to the notion that catering is a poor relation to restaurant cooking. Founded in 1980, her Barraud Caterers, Ltd offers clients sophisticated food presented with flair and imagination. Once a drama teacher, Rosemary says she enjoys catering because "it's like putting on a performance with a different cast and crew every night." Among her more spectacular productions: an ancient Roman meal commemorating the Ides of March.

Ken Stone

LUCIA HWONG

Lucia Hwong is a master of many arts in addition to those in the culinary sphere. A composer of music for theater, film, television, and the concert stage, she made her acclaimed Broadway debut as the composer of *M. Butterfly*. Her screen scores include *Year of the Dragon* and *Hiroshima*. She has produced two albums and has also been an on-screen presence in Bernardo Bertolucci's *The Last Emperor* and in the film *Lotus,* which she also scored. She is currently writing a ballet score for Ballet West and an opera for the Hallé Concerts Society in Manchester, England.

JONNA J. JENSEN
I CUGINI
1501 OCEAN AVENUE
· SANTA MONICA, CA 90401
310 451 4595

The creations of Jonna J. Jensen (no photo available), executive pastry chef at I Cugini restaurant in Santa Monica, California, reflect her Danish heritage but are strongly influenced by the freedom and spontaneity of California Cuisine, and by the abundance of produce available in California. Her experience includes stints with top restaurants, bakeries, and catering companies in California, Denmark, and France.

JEANNE JONES

An internationally respected food consultant and author, Jeanne Jones is an acknowledged pioneer of spa cuisine, having created menus for Canyon Ranch Fitness Resorts and Four Seasons Hotels, as well as authoring twenty-five cookbooks with an accent on health, most recently *Cook It Light Classics, Light and Hearty,* and *Cook It Light Desserts.*

Considered the "Dear Abby" of the food world, she writes a syndicated column that reaches 30 million readers each week.

KARINA KANSY

A native San Franciscan, Karina Kansky (no photo available) performs and composes music, designs clothes and jewelry, and brings the same creative spirit to the kitchen, where she likes to experiment with ingredients and presentations, believing firmly in the principle that "one feasts with the eyes first."

ED KASKY

Executive chef of Engine Co. No. 28, in downtown Los Angeles, Ed Kasky (no photo available) is recognized as a master of the grill, with a particular interest in updating and personalizing the classic dishes Mom used to make and the down-home favorites remembered from a New Jersey Shore childhood. In a career that alternated between acting and cooking, he committed himself wholeheartedly to food ten years ago, establishing himself as one of San Francisco's premier chefs before moving to L. A. and his present position in 1988.

VINCENT E. KIKUGAWA
PARADISE
889 WEST 190TH STREET
GARDENA, CA 90248
310 324 4800

PARADISE CAFE
4224 VINELAND AVENUE
NORTH HOLLYWOOD, CA 91602
818 985 6567

Vincent E. Kikugawa is the owner of Paradise, one of Los Angeles' premier eateries, and Paradise Cafe, located in Studio City, California. Prior to launching this successful venture, Kikugawa had held executive positions with several of America's leading restaurant chains including Charley Brown's Dinner Houses, W. R. Grace & Company, Marriott Corporation/ Host Division, and Hungry Tiger, Inc.

GEOFF LARSON
ALASKAN BREWING COMPANY
5429 SHAUNE DRIVE
JUNEAU, ALASKA 99801
907 780 5866

In partnership with his wife, Marcy, Chef and Brewmaster Geoff Larson

operates the Alaskan Brewing Company in Juneau. Geoff came to Alaska as a chemical engineer working for a mining company. After four years' intense study of the art of brewing, Geoff and Marcy did an internship in a microbrewery, then formulated their recipe for what became the award-winning Alaska Amber Beer, an instant classic that has since been joined by other fine brews such as a porter that is brewed from malts smoked over alderwood, an Alaskan specialty. Together, along with the "Alaskan Brew Crew," they have contributed their recipe for Autumn Apple-Potato Casserole.

MARK LATINO
CRESCENT CITY BREWHOUSE
527 DECATUR STREET
NEW ORLEANS, LA 70130
504 522 0571

Executive chef for New Orleans' Crescent City Brewhouse, Mark Latino (no photo available) is a native of the Big Easy who studied at the Culinary Institute of America before making his way back to Louisiana's premier brewpub by way of some of New York's most innovative kitchens.

JOSIE LeBALCH
SADDLE PEAK LODGE
419 COLD CANYON ROAD
CALABASAS, CA 91302
818 222 3888

Executive chef at Saddle Peak Lodge in Calabasas, California, Josie LeBalch (no photo available) has an extensive background in classical French and Venetian cooking and is a great proponent of cooking with beer. Given the current emphasis on lighter and more healthy food, she finds that beer—like wine and light stocks—can often be used in preference to oils and fats, and that it works as well as wine for poaching. Her creative approach to cooking can be found in her recipes for Intoxicated Quail and Venison Chops with Beer-Poached Pears.

PINO LUONGO
IL TOSCANACCIO
7 EAST 59TH STREET
NEW YORK, NY 10022
212 935 3535

Pino Luongo is a dynamic Florentine with a penchant for challenge and a perfectionist's concern with quality. An ambitious entrepreneur, he has created an impressive group of highly regarded restaurants, including Amarcord, Le Madri, mad.61, and Il Toscanaccio in New York, Cocco Pazzo in New York and Chicago, and Sapore di Mare in East Hampton, the last specializing in Italian seafood. For Le Madri (The Mothers) he brought in groups of Italian women from different regions to duplicate their native cuisines.

MANUEL MARES
GORDON BIERSCH
1625 ALVARADO STREET
SAN LEANDRO CA 94577
510 614 5450

Manuel Mares (no photo available) is chef at Hal's Bar & Grill, a Venice, California, gathering place for wheelers and dealers in the art community and representatives of the bohemian wing of show business. Having apprenticed at such established institutions as the Riviera Country Club, West Beach Café, and Jamaica Bay Inn, Mares is now gaining recognition as one of L.A.'s most creative chefs, gifted with the California talent for blending European and Pacific Rim elements into a unique cuisine.

CHEECH MARIN

The multitalented Cheech Marin (no photo available) is as innovative in the kitchen as he is on stage and screen. For fifteen years, he and his longtime partner, Tommy Chong, were one of the most successful comedy duos in America, showcasing their counterculture humor in movies, records, and concerts. Cheech and Chong teamed in eight feature films, the first of which, *Up in Smoke,* was the top-grossing comedy of 1978. On his own, Cheech Marin wrote, directed, and starred in the hit comedy *Born in East L.A.*

NOBU MATSUHISA

MATSUHISA
129 NORTH LA CIENEGA BOULEVARD
BEVERLY HILLS, CA 90211
310 659 9639

NOBU
105 HUDSON STREET
NEW YORK, NY 10013
212 219 0500

A critically acclaimed bicoastal Japanese chef, Matsuhisa came to prominence after opening sushi restaurants in Alaska and Peru. Working from a staggering repertoire of over 200 dishes, he launched his Matsuhisa restaurant in

Beverly Hills in 1987. More recently he followed this with Nobu (and partner Robert DeNiro), in New York's TriBeCa, which received a James Beard Award as best new restaurant of 1995. Rooted in Japanese cuisine, his menus nonetheless feature such Western delicacies as caviar, white truffles, and foie gras.

MAURIZIO MAZZON
IL FORNAIO
BEVERLY HILLS, BURLINGAME, COSTA MESA,
DEL MAR, IRVINE, PALO ALTO, PASADENA,
SAN FRANCISCO, SAN JOSE, AND
SACRAMENTO, CALIFORNIA

A native of the Veneto region of Italy, Maurizio Mazzon is a veteran of over twenty years of international restaurant experience, culminating in his present position as corporate executive chef for Il Fornaio, the San Francisco-based chain of restaurants and bakeries. Central to his training of other chefs in the organization are his *giro dei cuochi* (chef tours), during which he conducts small groups on trips through Italy seeking out new recipes to add to a library steeped in authenticity.

MICHAEL McCARTY
MICHAEL'S
1147 THIRD STREET
SANTA MONICA, CA 90403
310 451 0843

24 WEST 55TH STREET
NEW YORK, NY 10019
212 767 0555

In 1979, at the age of twenty-five, McCarty (no photo available) founded Michael's restaurant in Santa Monica, California, inaugurating the era of what would become known as "California Cuisine," a phenomenon based on an innovative amalgam of French, Italian, Hispanic, oriental, and native ingredients, techniques, presentations, and philosophies. Trained as a chef at the Cordon Bleu School in Paris, he is the author of *Michael's Cookbook: The Art of New American Food and Contemporary Entertaining from the Creator of Michael's Restaurant.*

PEGGY MELLODY

A resident of Los Angeles, Peggy Mellody is a consultant, writer, editor, and cooking instructor, whose work has earned her a reputation as a respected food authority. She is the author of *Sweet Celebrations* and *The*

Los Angeles Food Guide, as well as the co-author of *Cobblers, Crumbles, and Crisps* and *In the Chips: The Complete Chocolate Chip Cookbook.*

RICHARD MOSKOVITZ
DEERFIELD BEACH/BOCA RATON
HILTON HOTEL
100 FAIRWAY DRIVE
DEERFIELD, FL 33441
305 427 7700

Now serving as the Director of Culinary Operations for the Deerfield Beach/Boca Raton Hilton Hotel, Richard Moskovitz (no photo available) was previously executive chef for Carnival Cruise Lines, for which he was also Shoreside Food and Beverage Manager. Born and raised in Washington, D.C., he apprenticed there with the Potomac Restaurant Group and honed his skills as chef of the nationally acclaimed restaurant Nora.

WAYNE NISH
MARCH
405 EAST 58TH STREET
NEW YORK, NY 10022
215 754 6272

Wayne Nish inherited his love of cooking from his Maltese grandmother and his love for the exotic from his Japanese-Norwegian father. He apprenticed at the renowned Quilted Giraffe restaurant in New York when it was at the forefront of the transition from French nouvelle to truly American cuisine. He became executive chef at La Colombe d'Or in 1988, and in 1990 he opened his own Sutton Place restaurant, March, which quickly became a culinary mecca for diners from all over the world.

MICHAEL NIX
PESCE FRESCO/COPPER MOUNTAIN RESORT
209 TEN MILE CIRCLE
COPPER MOUNTAIN, CO 80443
970 968 2318

Like many ski resorts, Copper Mountain, Colorado, has become home to excellent restaurants, notably Pesce Fresco, located at the base of the ski slopes in the Copper Mountain Resort, where Chef Michael Nix has created an imaginative menu featuring fresh seafood dishes, pastas, and hearty soups. Nix belongs to the new breed of chefs who welcome the opportunity to experiment with ingredients that have been overlooked—such as beer—or that are borrowed from cuisines once thought of as exotic.

BRADLEY OGDEN
LARK CREEK INN
234 MAGNOLIA AVENUE
LARKSPUR, CA 94939
415 924 7766

ONE MARKET
1 MARKET STREET
SAN FRANCISCO, CA 94105
415 777 5577

As executive chef of the popular San Francisco restaurant known simply as One Market, and Lark Creek Cafe, Bradley Ogden also oversees the cooking at The Lark Creek Inn, which specializes in seasonal farm-fresh American country cooking. Called by Pierre Franey "one of the best American chefs on the scene," Ogden is also a cookbook author and has had input into American Airlines' food service, as well as serving as adviser for one of Euro Disney's American-style restaurants.

WILLIAM PRUNTY
JEAN–CLAUDE
137 SULLIVAN STREET
NEW YORK, NY 10012
212 475 9232

CAFE LURE
169 SULLIVAN STREET
NEW YORK, NY 10012
212 473 2642

Brooklyn-born William Prunty is a graduate of both the New York Restaurant School and the Culinary Institute of America. Following an apprenticeship in Frankfurt, Germany, he returned to New York to work for the well-known David Bouley. He became head chef at The Jean-Claude Restaurant in 1991 and recently opened Cafe Lure in New York, Jean-Claude's second restaurant, in 1995.

G. RICHARD POINTER
LA CASCADA RESTAURANT/
DOUBLETREE HOTEL
201 MARQUETTE N.W.
ALBUQUERQUE, NM 87102
505 247 3344

As executive chef of the La Cascada Restaurant, Doubletree Hotel Albuquerque, New Mexico, Chef Pointer specializes in Continental-modified Southwestern cuisine and Hawaiian fish dishes. He has been guest chef at the Hotel de Paris in Monaco, sous chef at the Hyatt Regency Hotel in Chicago, and executive chef at Bishop's Lodge in Santa Fe, New Mexico.

MARIE–CLAIRE QUITTELIER
BELGIUM TRADING COMPANY
P.O. BOX 4574
AUSTIN, TX 78756
512 323 5832

Born in Belgium, a country famous for its beer and chocolate, Marie-Claire was raised in a family of food enthusiasts and has made a career of passing on this enthusiasm. Chef and educator, she has mastered the art of elegant, easy, hassle-free entertaining with a European flair. Based in Austin, Texas, Marie-Claire conducts food seminars and cooking workshops and is also president of the Belgian Trading Company, which imports Belgian gourmet items and exports Texas specialties.

FAZ POURSOHI
FAZ RESTAURANTS
600 HARTZ AVENUE
DANVILLE CA 94526
510 838 1320

Faz Poursohi has been passionate about food since he was a child growing up in Tehran, Iran, where the table was always stocked with fresh produce from the family farm. Moving to America in 1974, he became involved in food professionally, and in 1986 he created the restaurant Circolo in San Francisco, then reopened the Southwestern-inspired Santa Fe Grill across the bay in Berkeley. Two other Poursohi restaurants—Faz Café and Faz Restaurant and Bar—provide San Francisco diners with Mediterranean food with a Middle Eastern accent.

MICHAEL ROBERTS
TWIN PALMS
101 WEST GREEN STREET
PASADENA, CA 91103
818 577 2567

A pioneer of California Cuisine when it emerged as a culinary force in the early 1980s, Michael Roberts is now chef and partner in Twin Palms, located in the picturesque Old Town section of Pasadena, California. Here Roberts has created a menu of rustic French Provençal food, emphasizing slow cooking as a way of blending and mellowing natural flavors. Honored by the James Beard Foundation as a Great Regional Chef, Roberts is the author of three cookbooks and contributes regularly to *Gourmet, Food & Wine,* and other publications.

ROBERT ROSENKRANZ

Chairman and controlling shareholder of Delphi Financial Group, a large insurance holding company, Robert Rosenkranz is an enthusiastic and accomplished amateur chef. A graduate of Yale University and Harvard Law School, Rosenkranz established the foundation that bears his name, which recently endowed the Rosenkranz Writer in Residence Program at Yale. He serves on the boards of Lincoln Center Theater, Lincoln Center Film Society, and the Manhattan Institute.

LIZI RUCH

Lizi Ruch is a graduate of the Parsons School of Design who has made a name for herself as a knitwear designer. Growing up in a food-loving Louisville family, she spent much of her early life in the kitchen developing a passion for cooking that matches her passion for style.

JOHN SCHLANER
MERV GRIFFIN'S RESORTS CASINO HOTEL
1133 BOARDWALK
ATLANTIC CITY, NJ 08401
609 344 6000

In the culinary field for twenty years, John Schlaner is executive chef of Merv Griffin's Resorts Casino Hotel, making him responsible for the company's nine restaurants, two of which have won the Zagat award for fine dining for three consecutive years. Chef Schlaner has been inducted into the American Academy of Chefs, the honor society of the American Culinary Foundation.

ERIC SCHLESINGER
WATERFRONT ALE HOUSE
136 ATLANTIC AVENUE
BROOKLYN. NY 11021
718 522 3794

A graduate of the Culinary Arts Institute, Eric Schlesinger cooked at several hotels (the Grand Hyatt, the St. Regis, and the United Nations Plaza, all in New York) and restaurants (Mesa Grill, Zoe, Iridium) before opening the Waterfront Ale House in Brooklyn in 1989.

A favorite "local" for the residents of Brooklyn Heights and Cobble Hill, the Waterfront Ale House serves an excellent range of beers and hearty food that emphasizes robust, up-front flavors.

Chip Simons

JOHN SEDLAR
ABIQUIU
1413 FIFTH STREET
SANTA MONICA, CA 90401
310 395 8611

John Sedlar's heritage is deeply rooted in the New Mexican pueblo of Abiquiu, where his great-grandparents maintained the family ranch, and it is after this pueblo that he has named his latest Santa Monica restaurant. After apprenticing himself to the legendary chef Jean Bertanou of L'ermitage, he opened his first restaurant, Saint Estephe, combining classic French cooking with touches of the Southwest. Afterward came the still highly regarded Bikini, in Los Angeles. Sedlar is the author of *Modern Southwest Cooking* and has been named to the First Annual Culinary Arts Hall of Fame Awards as one of the top ten chefs in America.

E. K. Waller

MICHAEL S. SHAFER
DEPOT AN URBAN GRILL ROOM & BAR
1250 CABRILLO AVENUE
TORRANCE, CA 90501
310 787 7501

European-trained chef Michael S. Shafer has cooked for presidents, heads of state, and royalty. In this country, he was executive sous chef at the Century Plaza Hotel in Los Angeles and is now chef/general manager of Depot An Urban Grill Room & Bar while also overseeing operations at Fino, Misto, and Chez Melange. Over the years, Chef Shafer has earned many culinary awards, including the Gold Medal at the 1988 Culinary Olympics in Frankfurt, Germany.

JOHN SOLA
DAILY GRILL
11677 SAN VICENTE BOULEVARD, 404
LOS ANGELES CA 90049
310 442 0044

THE GRILL
9560 DAYTON WAY
BEVERLY HILLS CA 90210
310 276 0615

A varied career in food has culminated in John Sola's position as executive chef with Grill Concepts of Beverly Hills. Mr. Sola created the menu and served as the first chef at The Grill in Beverly Hills, which, from its opening in 1984, became a mecca for discriminating eaters with a taste for imaginative brasserie-style food. Sola now oversees kitchen operations at all of the Daily Grills, offshoots of the Beverly Hills original, in Southern California.

Michael Mazzeo

CLAUDE-ALAIN SOLLIARD
RAOUL'S
180 PRINCE STREET
NEW YORK, NY 10012
212 966 3518

New York restaurants have long benefited from the skills of Swiss chefs, and one of the best is Claude-Alain Solliard, who is in charge of the kitchen at Raoul's in SoHo—a downtown favorite for twenty years—where he prepares hearty bistro fare with imagination and flair for diners who range from local artists and art dealers to Wall Street lawyers and bankers and uptown food cognoscenti.

ANDRÉ SOLTNER
LUTÈCE
249 EAST 50TH STREET
NEW YORK, NY 10022
212 752 2225

One of the most acclaimed French chefs in America, André Soltner was chef-proprietor of New York's legendary Lutèce restaurant from its inception in 1961 until his retirement in 1995. For four consecutive years, 1983 to 1987, it was named Critic's Choice as America's greatest restaurant, and Chef Soltner—who has won scores of awards for his dazzling culinary achievements—was chosen Chef of the Year in 1990 by Chefs In America, and in 1993 was awarded the James Beard Foundation Lifetime Achievement Award.

NORMAN STEWART

British-born Norman Stewart is one of the world's top food stylists. An accomplished chef in his own right, Stewart spent his early career cooking for the rich and famous and perfecting the presentation skills he now lavishes on cookbooks, magazine shoots, advertising campaigns, and movies.

SHIGEFUMI TACHIBE
CHAYA BRASSERIE
8741 ALDEN DRIVE
LOS ANGELES CA 90048
310 396 1179

CHAYA VENICE
110 NAVY STREET
VENICE, CA 90291
310 396 1179

At the age of fifteen, Chef Tachibe began training as a chef in Nagasaki, Japan, where he learned traditional French cuisine. He later served as exchange chef at Giannino restaurant in Milan, Italy. These experiences enabled him to perfect the fusion of styles he brought to California in 1981, introducing his innovative California-Pacific Rim food at La Petite Chaya in Los Angeles. After rave reviews, two other restaurants followed—Chaya Brasserie and Chaya Venice—with executive chef Tachibe continuing to refine the Chaya style.

Illustration by Kent Twitchell

TAMARA THOMAS

As president of Fine Arts Services, based in Los Angeles, Tamara Thomas is an acknowledged expert in the field of public art and corporate collecting who has purchased artwork and provided ancillary services for a variety of public agencies and major corporations in twenty states. By avocation, however, she is a gifted cook who likes to entertain friends and clients with dishes that emphasize unusual combinations of ingredients.

Gary Leonard, Downtown News

TARA THOMAS
410 BOYD
410 BOYD STREET
LOS ANGELES, CA 90013
213 617 2491

During the twelve years since Tara Thomas has been in the hospitality industry, she has served as apprentice in the venerable Trattoria Blasut in Lavorino, Italy, worked as a liaison for hospitality and public relations at two important California wineries, and has been on the team that launched one of San Francisco's finest hotels. All this has culminated in her present position as chef and co-owner of the successful and critically acclaimed 410 Boyd restaurant in downtown Los Angeles.

JAMES D. THOMPSON
HOTEL MEXICO
792 EASTGATE SOUTH DRIVE
CINCINNATI, OH 45245
513 753 4000

James D. Thompson has been associated with some of the more successful Mexican-oriented restaurant concepts of the recent past, including Chi-Chi's Mexican restaurants in New York, Florida, and Indianapolis, Hooters/Two Pesos Mexican Café in Virginia Beach, and currently Hotel Mexico in Cincinnati, which is described as a combination of neo-Jurassic, New Age, nature, and science with hospitality and fresh food.

Mary Randlett

JERRY TRAUNFELD
THE HERBFARM
32804 ISSAQUAH-FALL CITY ROAD
FALL CITY, WA 98024
206 784 2222

By the age of fifteen, Jerry Traunfeld had catered a wedding for 100 guests. Inspired to pursue a career in cooking, he graduated from the California Culinary Institute, then spent several years in San Francisco before relocating to the Northwest. He is now chef at the The Herbfarm in Fall City, Washington, which has been featured in the *New York Times, Food & Wine, Gourmet,* and *Bon Appétit.* At The Herbfarm, Traunfeld creates each week's six- or nine-course menu as well as oversees the extensive kitchen garden.

ROBERT ULMANN
GREAT LAKES BREWING COMPANY
2516 MARKET STREET
CLEVELAND, OH 44113
216 771 4404

Chef Ulmann is in charge of the kitchens at the Great Lakes Brewing Company's colorful Victorian saloon and brewpub in Cleveland, Ohio. (Honest-to-God bullet holes in the antique bar.) Great Lakes beers enjoy an enviable reputation in the craft brewing world and Rob Ulmann takes pride in making his bistro-style dishes a worthy complement to the Conway brothers' Dortmunder Gold and Moon Dog Ale.

ANN WALKER
ANN WALKER CATERING, INC.
5627B PARADISE DRIVE
CORTE MADERA, CA 94925
415 945 0952

Food educator, writer, and restaurant consultant, Ann Walker also heads Ann Walker Catering, Inc., located in Corte Madera, California. Her San Rafael restaurant, Café Tango, which she ran from 1986 to 1989, was the first tapas restaurant on the West Coast. Walker's approach to food is eclectic, and she travels frequently to Europe and Latin America conducting on-the-spot research. Her books include *Tequila: the Book, Tapas: The Book,* and *Best of California.*

ISLES AND RICHARD WALLACE
REDHOOK BREWERY
14300 N. E. 145TH STREET
WOODINVILLE, WA 98072
206 483 3232

Isles and Richard Wallace have been cooking together for eighteen years, the last five as caterers for Redhook Brewery's Trolleyman Pub in the Fremont section of Seattle, an assignment that helped to heighten their interest in cooking with beer. Recently the Wallaces became chefs for Redhook's new and much larger Forecaster's Public House in Woodinville, Washington.

BARRY WINE

Barry Wine is celebrated as the founder of the Quilted Giraffe, acknowledged for almost two decades to be one of America's best and most innovative restaurants. Today, he operates in cyberspace, routing food professionals and afficionados alike to the information superhighway by means of his Restaurant City Service, available through the Wide World Web.

DIANE ROSSEN WORTHINGTON

Diane Rossen Worthington is the author of eight cookbooks and is considered an expert on modern California Cuisine. Her latest cookbooks include *The California Cook* and *Diner.* In addition, she is a two-time consecutive James Beard Award-winning talk radio show host on food in Los Angeles.

ALBERTA WRIGHT
JEZEBEL
630 NINTH AVENUE
NEW YORK, NY 10036
212 582 1045

Alberta Wright's (no photo available) innovative home-style Southern cooking forms the basis of the cuisine at the popular Jezebel restaurant in New York. She has loved to cook since childhood, when she would often take a chicken from her mother's yard and cook it in the woods for her friends. She has borrowed traditional recipes learned from the female members of her family and enhanced them with ingredients encountered during her extensive travels to create an eclectic and personal repertoire.

JIM YOUNG
HOLLYWOOD ATHLETIC CLUB
1000 UNIVERSAL CENTER DRIVE, SUITE 208
UNIVERSAL CITY, CA 91608
818 505 9238

Satisfying the appetites of discriminating diners at the Hollywood Athletic Club in Universal CityWalk has proved to be a stimulating challenge for recently appointed executive chef Jim Young. A graduate of the Culinary Institute of America, with a résumé that boasts service at such notable Los Angeles restaurants as Maple Drive, Champagne, and Nicky Blair's, Young specializes in a cuisine that combines French and Italian influences with stylish California eclecticism.

SUBSTITUTION CHART

STYLES	BREWERY	MALT	HOP	COMMENTS
ALES				
Pale and amber ales—which can in fact be amber or ruby red in color—are the clarets of the beer world and should be cooked much as you would cook with a fine Bordeaux. Their malt character adds flavor to any meat dish, but since some of these brews are very hoppy, the chef must be careful to compensate for their bitterness.	Alaska Amber Ale	Medium	Medium +	
	Anchor Liberty Ale	Medium	Medium	
	Anchor Steam	Medium -	Medium	
	Anderson Valley Boont Amber Ale	Medium	Medium	
	Bass Ale	Medium -	Medium -	
	Dixie Blackened Voodoo	Medium	Medium	
	Full Sail Amber Ale	Medium	Medium +	
	Great Lakes Burning River Ale	Medium	High	
Pale Ales	Hops-Jack Rabbit Pale Ale	Medium	Medium	
Blonde Ales	Mendocino's Red Tail Ale	Medium	Medium +	
Amber Ales	Merchant du Vin-The Pikes Pale	Medium +	High	
American Ales	New Amsterdam Ale	Medium	Medium	
Alt Style	New Belgium-Fat Tire Amber Ale	Medium	Medium	
	Pete's Wicked Ale	Medium	Medium	
	Pyramid Pale Ale	Medium	Medium +	
	Red Hook (ESB)	Medium	High	
	Red Stallion-Crescent City	Medium	Medium	
	Rhino Chasers American Amber Ale	Medium	Medium	
	Samuel Smith Pale Ale	Medium	Medium	
	Saranac-Adirondack Amber Ale	Medium	Medium	
	Saranac Pale Ale	Medium	Medium -	
	Sierra Nevada Pale Ale	Medium	High	
	St. Stans Alt	Medium	Medium	
	Wild Goose Amber	Medium	Medium	
	Wynkoop Railyard Ale	Medium	Medium	
BROWN ALES				
Brown ales are the burgundies of the beer world. They can be substituted for pale ale in many meat dishes, and have a special affinity for rich stews, for game, and for cheese dishes.	Brooklyn Brown Ale	Medium	Medium	
	Pyramid Best Brown	Medium	Medium	
	Samuel Smith Nut Brown Ale	Medium	Medium	

STYLES	BREWERY	MALT	HOP	COMMENTS
SCOTCH ALE				
Scotch Ale can be used in any dish that calls for brown ale, especially if you want to accentuate the malt character.	*Rogue Scotch Ale*	*High*	*Medium*	
WHEAT ALES				
Wheat beer is best suited to use in dishes with a delicate flavor. Fish braised in wheat beer can be delicious, and wheat beer makes a fine base for a veal stew. Belgian lambic wheat beers are especially useful in salad dressings, having no hop bitterness.	*Ayinger-Bräu-Weisse*	*Low+*	*Low*	
	Celis White	*Medium*	*Light*	*Coriander and Curacao*
	Lindeman's Cuvée René (Gueuze Lambic)	*High*	—	*High acidity*
	New Belgium Sunshine Wheat	*Medium*	*Medium -*	
	Pyramid Hefeweizen	*Medium -*	*Medium -*	
	Wheathook	*Medium -*	*Medium -*	
	Tabernash-Weiss	*Medium*	*Low +*	
	Wynkoop-Wilderness Wheat	*Medium*	—	
FRUIT BEERS				
The classic fruit beers are members of the Belgian lambic family—spontaneously fermented wheat beers in which cherries, raspberries, or other fruit has been macerated. They add much to certain desserts, as do the various American fruit beers—usually wheat-based—which have recently come onto the market.	*Celis Raspberry*	*Medium*	*Light*	
	Dixie White Mouse	*Medium -*	*Low*	
	Lindemans Framboise (Raspberry)	*Medium*	—	
	Lindemans Kriek (Cherry)	*Medium*	—	
	Lindemans Peche (Peach)	*Medium*	—	
	Rhino Chasers Peach Honey Wheat	*Medium*	*Medium -*	
	Thomas Kemper Apricot Ale	*Medium*	*Medium*	
SMOKED BEERS				
Smoked beers are a specialty of Franconia, though fine versions are now brewed in America. They have an affinity for ham and charcuterie of all kinds, as well as for cheese dishes.	*Alaska Smoked Porter*	*High*	*Medium*	*Smokey flavor*
	Kaiserdom Rauchbier	*High -*	*Medium +*	*Smokey flavor*
	Rhino Chasers Smoked Porter	*High*	*Medium*	*Smokey flavor*

STYLES	BREWERY	MALT	HOP	COMMENTS
BELGIAN ALES *There are many kinds of Belgian ale, but typically they are strong, very malty, and very hoppy. Superb in stews, they are also excellent in game dishes and in the more robust kind of meat dishes. Because they are so malty and so hoppy, however, special care must be taken with these brews or they will overpower the other ingredients. (The alcohol itself evaporates in the process of cooking, but it is the high proportion of malt to water that gives these beers both their richness of flavor and their high alcohol content.)*	*Chimay* *Orval Trappist Ale* *Saint Sixtus (Belgium Abbey Ale)*	*Medium-High* *Medium* *High +*	*Medium-High* *High +* *Medium*	*High acidity* *High acidity* *High acidity*
PORTERS *These delectable black beers can be used interchangeably with stout for cooking purposes, though they are generally a little lighter bodied and more delicate than the typical stout. Poultry braised in porter can be delicious.*	*Anchor Porter* *BlackHook Porter*	*High +* *High +*	*Medium +* *Medium +*	
BARLEY WINES *These strong specialty ales are similar in character to Belgian ales and should be used with the same respect.*	*Anchor Barley Wine* *Sierra Nevada Barley Wine*	*High +* *High +*	*High* *High*	
STNTS *These inky black brews are rich and creamy. Generally they are also very generously hopped, though sweet versions—such as Mackeson from England—can be found and are very useful in the kitchen. As with Belgian ales and Barley wines, stouts add much to rich meat and game dishes, and even to some fish dishes*	*Brooklyn Stout* *Marin Brewing San Quentin Stout* *Mendocino-Black Hawk Stout* *Merchant Du Vin* *Pike Place XXXXX Stout* *Oldenberg Brewing Company- Frederick Hauch Centennial Stout* *Rhino Chasers Espresso Stout* *Samuel Adams Creme Stout*	*High +* *High +* *High +* *High +* *High +* *High -* *Medium* *High +*	*Medium +* *High* *Medium +* *Medium +* *High* *Medium +* *Medium* *Medium +*	

STYLES	BREWERY	MALT	HOP	COMMENTS
such as stewed eel, but the bitterness of Guinness-style stouts must be compensated for.	Samuel Smith Celebrated Oatmeal Stout	Medium	Medium -	
	Samuel Smith Imperial Stout	High +	Medium +	
	Saranac Stout	Medium -	Medium +	
	Watney's Creme Stout	High +	Medium +	
WINTER ALE Winter ales are strong seasonal brews, often quite spicy, that should be used like Belgian ales or barley wine.	Rhino Chasers Winterful	Medium +	Medium +	
LIGHTER STYLE LAGERS These supermarket staples are thirst quenchers at best and will add very little character to food.	Beck's	Light	Light	
	Carta Blanca	Light	Light	
	Corona	Light	Light	
	Heineken	Light	Light	
	Kirin	Light	Light	
	Rolling Rock	Light +	Light +	
AMBER LIGHTS These lighter-bodied Viennese-style beers have some roast malt character that will lend delicate flavor to fish and poultry.	Bohemia	Light	Light	
	Dos Equis	Light	Light	
	Modelo Negro	Light	Light	
LAGERS, PILSNERS, VIENNA LAGERS, DARK LAGERS As a general rule, pale lagers are most useful when cooking fish or poultry, though some of them are robust enough to use with red meat. In general, though, amber and dark lagers—also known as Vienna-style lagers and dunkels—are more suited to red meat. They can be used in much the same way as pale ales and brown ales and often have the added advantage of being less hoppy and therefore easier to cook with. Be warned, though, that authentic pilsners tend to be very hoppy.	Brooklyn Lager	Medium	Medium	
	Celis Golden	Medium -	Medium	
	Dixie Brewing Lager	Light +	Light +	
	Full Sail Golden	Medium	Medium	
	Gordon Biersch Dunkel	Medium +	Medium -	
	Great Lakes Eliot Ness Vienna Lager	Medium	Medium	
	Perry's Majestic Lager	Medium	Medium -	
	Pete's Gold Coast Lager	Medium -	Medium	
	Moretti	Medium -	Light +	
	Rhino Chasers Lager	Medium	Medium	
	Rhino Chasers Dark Roasted Läger	Medium +	Medium +	
	Stoudt's Pils	Medium -	Medium	
	Tabernash-Denargo Lager	Medium	Medium -	

STYLES	BREWERY	MALT	HOP	COMMENTS
BOCKS *Bocks are strong lagers that can be used in much the same way as high gravity ales such as barley wine, but bocks tend to be less bitter than equivalently strong ales and are therefore easier to cook with.*	*Ayinger Maibock* *Celis Pale Bock* *Einbecker Ur-Bock* *Sierra Nevada Pale Bock*	*Medium +* *Medium* *Medium* *Medium*	*Medium* *Medium +* *Medium* *Medium*	
DOPPEL (DOUBLE) BOCKS *Doppelbocks are very strong, very malty, and very tricky to cook with since they have the tendency to overpower other ingredients. Still, they have their place in rich stews and in some cheese and savory dishes*	*Ayinger Celebrator Doppelbock* *Samuel Adams Tripple Bock* *Stout Honey Double Bock*	*High* *High* *High*	*High* *Low* *Medium +*	*Like a port or sherry* *Slight honey in finish*

MEASUREMENTS

LIQUID MEASURES

1	dash	= 6	drops
1	teaspoon	= ⅓	tablespoon
1	tablespoon	= ½	fluid ounce
4	tablespoon	= ¼	cup
5 ⅓	tablespoons	= ⅓	cup
8	tablespoons	= ½	cup
16	tablespoons	= 1	cup *(dry)*
1	fluid ounce	= 2	tablespoons
16	fluid ounces	= 1	pint
1	cup *(liquid)*	= ½	pint
1	cup	= 16	tablespoons
1	cup	= 8	fluid ounces
2	cups	= 1	pint
2	pints	= 1	quart
4	quarts	= 1	gallon
16	ounces *(dry)*	= 1	pound

DRY MEASURES

1	dash	= less than ⅛ teaspoon	
1	teaspoon	= ⅓ tablespoon	
1	tablespoon	= 3 teaspoons	
¼	cup	= 4 tablespoons	
⅓	cup	= 5 tablespoons + 1 teaspoon	
½	cup	= 8 tablespoons	
⅔	cup	= 10 tablespoons + 2 teaspoons	
¾	cup	= 12 tablespoons	
1	cup	= 16 tablespoons	

VEGETABLES AND FRUITS

Apple	*(1 medium)*	= 1	cup, *chopped*
Avocado	*(1 medium)*	= 1	cup, *mashed*
Broccoli	*(1 stalk)*	= 2	cups florets
Cabbage	*(1 large)*	= 10	cups, *chopped*
Carrot	*(1 medium)*	= ½	cup, *diced*
Celery	*(3 stalks)*	= 1	cup, *diced*
Eggplant	*(1 medium)*	= 4	cups, *cubed*
Lemon	*(1 medium)*	= 2	tablespoons juice
Onion	*(1 medium)*	= 1	cup, *diced*
Orange	*(1 medium)*	= ½	cup juice
Parsley	*(1 bunch)*	= 3	cups, *chopped*
Spinach	*(fresh)*, 12 cups, *loosely packed*		
		= 1	cup, *cooked*
Tomato	*(1 medium)*	= ¾	cup, *diced*
Zucchini	*(1 medium)*	= 2	cups, *diced*

1 lemon	= 2–3 tablespoons juice and 2 teaspoons zest
1 orange	= 6–8 tablespoons juice and 2–3 tablespoons zest
1 cup heavy cream	= 2 cups whipped cream
2 cups water	= 1 pound

GLOSSARY

ADDITIVES

Additives are elements such as enzymes and preservatives that are often used by large brewers for such purposes as lengthening shelf-life or providing the brew with an artificial head. Such chemical and biological additives are shunned by craft brewers.

ADJUNCTS

Adjuncts are a special category of additive in the form of different kinds of grain added to the barley malt during the brewing process. Cheap adjuncts such as corn make for an inferior beer. Certain adjuncts such as wheat and oatmeal contribute to authentic specialty brews.

ALCOHOL

Alcohol is a colorless, volatile, flammable liquid produced by the fermentation of certain carbohydrates (grains, especially malted barley, in the case of beer). Typical American and European beers contain about 4 to 5 percent alcohol by volume, but strong brews such as barley wines or bocks may be significantly higher in alcohol content, though very few beers exceed 10 percent alcohol by volume. Pure alcohol boils at 173°F., water at 212°F. Since beer is a mixture of water and alcohol, its boiling point will be somewhere between these two temperatures, depending on its strength; but when cooking with beer (or any other form of alcoholic beverage), all the alcohol will have evaporated when the mixture is heated to 212°F.

ALE

A beer made with top-fermenting yeast.

ALL MALT

An all-malt beer is a beer made from 100 percent barley malt without additives or adjuncts.

ANAHEIM CHILE PEPPER

A number of recipes in this book call for both beer and chile peppers and, just as the beer selected influences the dish, so does the kind of chile chosen. Anaheim chile peppers are long and thin, normally medium green in color, and relatively mild. A red version is sometimes called New Mexico red chile.

ANCHO CHILE PEPPER

These dried chile peppers are a rich, reddish brown in color, like a beer brewed from roasted malt. They can be mild, but some are quite spicy

ARBORIO RICE

An Italian rice that is used in the preparation of risotto, its short, chubby grains are very high in starch content, which provides the risotto with the desired creamy texture.

BARLEY

The basic grain of brewing.

BARLEY WINE

A strong form of ale.

BIERWORST

A cooked sausage, of German origin, dark reddish in color and distinctively garlicky.

BOCK

A strong form of German lager. In other countries, the term "bock"—German for billy goat—is used more loosely.

BOTTLE-CONDITIONED

A bottle-conditioned beer is an unpasteurized craft beer, belonging to the ale family, which contains active yeast, meaning that it is still "live" until the bottle is uncapped.

BRAISE

This is a method of preparing food that lends itself well to cooking with beer. Food is first browned in fat, then cooked in a tightly covered vessel in a small amount of liquid.

BRATWURST

A staple of German cuisine, this form of sausage is made from highly seasoned pork and veal.

BRAUNSCHWEIGER

A smoked liver sausage, enriched with milk and eggs, named for the German town of Braunschweig.

CARBON DIOXIDE

Carbon dioxide gas is produced naturally during the brewing process and causes a degree of carbonation that varies from one style of beer to another. Big commercial brewers often pump extra carbon dioxide into their brews to promote added effervescence.

CASK-CONDITIONED

A cask-conditioned beer is an unpasteurized craft beer belonging to the ale family, which has undergone a secondary fermentation in the cask and is still "live" when the cask is tapped.

CHILI PASTE

A staple of Chinese cuisine, this paste is a blend of fermented fava beans, flour, red chile peppers, and garlic. It can be found ready-made in Chinese groceries and some supermarkets.

CHIPOTLE CHILE PEPPER

This hot form of chile pepper is often used in the preparation of stews and sauces. It can be purchased dried or canned, and a pickled version is sometimes served as an hors d'oeuvre.

CHORIZO

A coarse, highly seasoned sausage that is a staple of both Spanish and Mexican cooking. The Spanish version is made from smoked pork, the Mexican version from fresh pork.

CONTRACT BREW

A contract brew is a beer brewed for an entrepreneur, to his formula, by a brewery he does not own. Several excellent craft beers are now produced this way.

DEGLAZE

This is a technique that is valuable when cooking with beer. After food has been sautéed, and the food and excess fat have been removed from the pan, deglazing is achieved by pouring a small amount of liquid into the hot pan and stirring to loosen the morsels of browned food adhering to the bottom. This is often done with stock or wine, but it can be done equally well with beer. The resulting mixture provides a tasty base for a sauce to accompany the sautéed food.

DOPPELBOCK

A very strong, usually sweetish, German beer.

FATBACK

The layer of fat—usually sold unsalted—taken from the back of a pig. Not to be confused with salt pork, which is taken from the pig's flanks and belly.

FERMENTATION

The process by which yeast organisms convert sugars into alcohol and carbon dioxide.

FLOWERS

Edible flowers, sometimes used in cooking or as a garnish, include nasturtiums, violets, jasmine, marigolds, daisies, geraniums, chamomile, lilacs, chrysanthemums, pansies, violas, and apple and almond blossoms. Never use flowers bought at the florist, since the chances are these have been sprayed with insecticide. It is safest to buy flowers grown specifically for the kitchen. These can be found in gourmet stores and some health food stores.

GARAM MASALA

A staple of Indian cookery, garam masala is a blend of ground dry-roasted spices sometime sprinkled on food during the cooking process, sometimes shortly before serving. There is no single approved mix of spices that makes up the garam masala (literally "warm mixture"). It can be very mild or relatively hot, but typically it will include black pepper, chili powder, cloves, cumin, cardamom, cinnamon, ginger, nutmeg, fennel, mace, turmeric, and coriander. Good commercial garam masalas can be found in some supermarkets and all Indian specialty stores.

HOPS

The female flowers of the hop vine (*humulus lupus*) are used to provide beer with flavor, bitterness, and aroma.

They also help preserve the brew.

JALAPEÑO CHILE PEPPER

Dark green chile peppers, about 2 inches long and up to 1 inch in diameter. These peppers should be handled with care since they come in only two versions, hot to very hot, and their seeds and veins are fiercely hot.

KNACKWURST/KNOCKWURST

Garlicky short links of beef and/or pork sausage, often served with sauerkraut.

LAGER

A beer made with a bottom-fermenting yeast.

NLT

This is a grain—usually barley—that has been soaked with water, permitted to sprout, then dried in a kiln and finally ground. It is from this raw material, mixed with water, that beer is brewed (see page 00). Sometimes malts are roasted, to a greater or lesser extent, a process that makes for darker beers, often with a roasted coffee flavor. Powdered malt and malt extract (a sweet, heavy syrup) are also used in the preparation of food, especially when cooking with beer. Powdered malt and malt extract can be found in health food stores and some supermarkets.

MICROBREWERY

This term describes a small craft brewery. At one time a microbrewery was defined as a brewery producing not more than 15,000 barrels a year. This definition is outdated, however, since a number of the breweries that defined what "micro" stood for now greatly exceed that annual production.

PASTEURIZATION

Pasteurization describes the process by which heat is used to end the activity of micro-organisms in a chemical process. In the case of beer, pasteurization—favored by most large commercial breweries—means that the brewing process has come to an end. Many craft beers are unpasteurized.

PHYLLO

A form of pastry originating in the eastern Mediterranean, it is made up of paper-thin leaves of dough. It can be found fresh in Greek and Middle Eastern stores, and frozen in many supermarkets.

PILSNER/PILSENER

A light, refreshing form of lager.

POACH

The technique of poaching—cooking food unhurriedly in liquid that is just at the boiling point or a little below—works well when the liquid is beer, which adds a distinctive character to any dish prepared this way.

POBLANO CHILE PEPPER

A large, dark green chile that when dried becomes known as Ancho chile pepper (q.v.). Poblanos are mild to medium-hot and the darkest examples—which are almost black—are the fullest in flavor.

PORTER

A dark—almost black—beer of the ale family, similar to stout but lighter in body.

REDUCE

The art of reducing—boiling a liquid so that it is diminished and thickened by evaporation—is important to the chef who cooks with beer, since it is a means of obtaining an enriched mixture that intensifies the flavor of the malt.

REINHEITSGEBOT

This is the Bavarian purity law which, since 1516, has dictated that all Bavarian beer (with the exception of wheat beers) be made from nothing but barley malt, yeast, water, and hops. The law was later adopted throughout Germany and is often voluntarily adhered to by craft brewers in other countries.

RENDER

A term used to describe the melting of animal fat over low heat so that it separates from the tissue to which it is attached. The melted fat can be further clarified by straining it through a cheesecloth or a paper filter.

ROUX

There are three basic kinds of roux—white, blond, and brown—each of which is a blend of flour and fat cooked slowly over a low flame and used to thicken soups, sauces, and other mixtures. White and blond roux are made with butter. Brown roux can be made with butter, with beef or pork drippings, or with various other kinds of fat such as rendered lard.

SERRANO CHILE PEPPER

A small, hot chile pepper that begins life a bright green color, then turns first red then yellow. Serrano chiles can be found fresh, canned, packed in oil, or pickled.

STOUT

A dark—almost black—beer of the ale family, similar to

porter but more full-bodied.

WATER BATH
A cooking technique that consists of placing a container (a soufflé dish, for example) in a shallow pan of warm water, thus surrounding the food with gentle heat. This method is called for when cooking delicate dishes such as custards.

YEAST
Micro-organisms of the fungus family that are used to ferment beer.

ZYMURGY
The branch of chemistry dealing with fermentation, hence the science of brewing.

FOR FURTHER READING

AMERICA'S BEST BEERS
Christopher Finch & W. Scott Griffiths
(Little, Brown and Company, New York, NY, 1994).

A BEER DRINKER'S COMPANION
Alan Eames
(Ayers Rock Press, Harvard, MA, 1986).

BEER: A CONNOISSEUR'S GUIDE
TO THE WORLD'S BEST
Christopher Finch
(Abbeville Press, New York, NY, 1989).

BEER AND GOOD FOOD
Myra Waldo
(Doubleday, New York, NY, 1958).

BREW CUISINE:
COOKING WITH BEER
Judith Gould and Ruth Koretsky
(Summerhill Press, Toronto, Canada, 1989).

BREWERY ADVENTURES
IN THE WILD WEST
Jack Erickson
(Redbrick Press, Reston, VA, 1989).

COOKING WITH BEER
Carol Fahy
(Drake Publishers, New York, NY, 1972).

ON TAP: THE GUIDE TO U.S. BREWPUBS
Steve Johnson
(WBR Publications, Clemson, SC, 1991).

REAL BEER AND GOOD EATS: THE REBIRTH OF
AMERICA'S BEER AND FOOD TRADITIONS
Bruce Aidells & Denis Kelly
(Alfred A. Knopf, Inc., New York, NY, 1992).

THE BEER MAKES IT BETTER COOKBOOK
Maria Russel and Mazine Stromberg
(Simon & Schuster, New York, NY, 1971).

THE ESSENTIALS OF BEER STYLE:
A CATALOG OF CLASSIC BEER STYLES
FOR BREWERS AND BEER ENTHUSIASTS
Fred Eckhardt
(Fred Eckhardt Associates, Portland, OR, 1989).

THE GOURMET GUIDE TO BEER
Howard Hillman
(Facts on File, New York, NY, 1987).

THE NEW WORLD GUIDE TO BEER
Michael Jackson
(Running Press Book Publishers, Philadelphia, PA 1988).

THE TASTE OF SUMMER
Diane Rossen Worthington
(Bantam Books, New York, NY 1988).

INDEX